What Your Colleagues /

To say I have been waiting for this book by Lisa Westman with great anticipation would be an understatement. She was a frequent and very popular guest blogger for my Finding Common Ground blog. Westman has hit it out of the park with her new book, much like she did with each and every guest blog. She has a deeply engaging writing style that offers practical steps on how to differentiate using her deep knowledge on the topic. She literally differentiated this book in a variety of ways to help us deepen our understanding. Not only is this a must-read, but it is a book that will be relevant for a very long time.

—Peter DeWitt
Author/Consultant

This book by Lisa Westman is a must-read for educators everywhere. She delivers a new look at how differentiation must work in our classrooms, with an emphasis on the concept of "student-driven differentiation," in which the focus is always on student learning, student growth, and investing students in their own learning and their own learning needs. This book is extremely well written and provides practical tips for teachers hoping to transform learning in their classrooms to ensure that all students learn at high levels. The tools and resources in this book—combined with Westman's expert insights—provide a road map for readers to better meet the needs of all students in our schools. Student-Driven Differentiation: 8 Steps to Harmonize Learning in the Classroom *is a game changer for educators—and the students they serve!*

—Jeffrey Zoul
Instructional and Leadership Coach, Speaker, Author

This fascinating book presents differentiation in a way that demystifies the strategy so that teachers can unlock thinking and promote rigorous instruction.

—Marian White-Hood, Head of School
Potomac Preparatory Public Charter School, Washington, DC

A step-by-step guide to differentiation—all educators need to read this book. It presents a clear and careful blueprint for an insightful and practical foundation in differentiation. When it comes to differentiation, educators have been looking for a practical book: Now we have it.

—Lyne N. Ssebikindu, Principal
Crump Elementary School, Cordova, TN

Lisa Westman does an excellent job of explaining the what of differentiation as well as the how. Examples from practitioners show it can be done effectively. The variety of voices—students, administrators, teachers, community—lends credibility by approaching differentiation from multiple perspectives. An excellent book to help teachers truly understand how to differentiate. Westman focuses on real-world examples that are driven by research and student needs.

—Jennifer Marten, Gifted & Talented Coordinator, Online School Coordinator

Plymouth Joint School District, Plymouth, WI

Lisa Westman hits a homerun with this practical and powerful book about learning, teaching, and excellence for ALL students. Containing examples from the field, blended with Lisa's courageous and proven success as a teacher leader, all who read this book will be able to implement student-focused strategies. This is a book all teachers and educational leaders need to read and share.

—Michael Lubelfeld, Author and Superintendent

Deerfield Public School District 109, Deerfield, IL

Westman shows the importance of focusing on the learner. She does this eloquently by supporting educators with practical ideas to empower students in their learning. Empowering learners should be the norm in education, and Westman helps educators move toward that standard.

—George Couros, Innovative Teaching, Learning, and Leadership Consultant

Author of *The Innovator's Mindset*

Lisa Westman presents a seamless alignment of differentiation strategies with approaches designed to empower students. She expertly weaves research, anecdotes, and personal stories with pragmatic and helpful how-tos. Her specific examples and graphics provide concrete visual tools to support the powerful professional growth opportunities she offers. I recommend this insightful, well-written book for teachers, teacher-leaders, instructional coaches, curriculum supervisors, and administrators.

—Debbie Silver, Author of *Fall Down 7 Times, Get Up 8, Deliberate Optimism,* and *Teaching Kids to Thrive*

Student-Driven
DIFFERENTIATION

LISA WESTMAN

FOREWORD BY CAROL ANN TOMLINSON

Student-Driven
DIFFERENTIATION

8 Steps to HARMONIZE
LEARNING in
the Classroom

CORWIN

A SAGE Publishing Company

FOR INFORMATION:

Corwin
A SAGE Company
2455 Teller Road
Thousand Oaks, California 91320
(800) 233-9936
www.corwin.com

SAGE Publications Ltd.
1 Oliver's Yard
55 City Road
London EC1Y 1SP
United Kingdom

SAGE Publications India Pvt. Ltd.
B 1/I 1 Mohan Cooperative Industrial Area
Mathura Road, New Delhi 110 044
India

SAGE Publications Asia-Pacific Pte. Ltd.
3 Church Street
#10-04 Samsung Hub
Singapore 049483

Acquisitions Editor: Ariel Bartlett Curry
Development Editor: Desirée A. Bartlett
Editorial Assistant: Jessica Vidal
Production Editor: Amy Schroller
Copy Editor: Lana Todorovic-Arndt
Typesetter: C&M Digitals (P) Ltd.
Proofreader: Dennis W. Webb
Indexer: Maria Sosnowski
Cover Designer: Candice Harman
Marketing Manager: Brian Grimm

Printed in the United States of America

ISBN 978-1-5063-9657-6

This book is printed on acid-free paper.

Certified Chain of Custody
Promoting Sustainable Forestry
www.sfiprogram.org
SFI-01268

SFI label applies to text stock

18 19 20 21 22 10 9 8 7 6 5 4 3 2 1

Contents

Part I: Foundation 1

Chapter 1: Relationships Come First 3

Chapter 2: Differentiation Is What Happens When Teachers Focus on Student Growth 15

Chapter 3: Four Areas to Differentiate 29

Chapter 8: The Role of Choice in Meeting Learning Intentions   131

Chapter 9: Your Journey With Student-Driven Differentiation   155

List of Online Tools and Resources

Downloadable versions of these tools and resources can be accessed on the companion website at http://resources.corwin.com/studentdrivendifferentiation.

Foreword

What If . . .

Lisa Westman is a deep thinker about classrooms, and a creative one. Her work is a catalyst for her readers (including this one) to think more deeply and more imaginatively about the work we do in the name of education. She causes us to ask, "What if . . ."

What if we began every school year, and every day in every school year, with the resolve to learn more about each student we teach? And what if we understood that knowledge to be the underpinning of everything else we seek to accomplish in our classrooms?

What if we accepted that a teacher building a positive and respectful relationship with each student was the precursor to their success as learners—and ours as teachers?

What if we could recall the profound joy and fulfillment a baby or a toddler or a child in the summer outdoors derives from learning? And what if we sought day after day, unit after unit, standard after standard to make our classrooms—no matter the age of our students—places where that joy and satisfaction are consistently palpable?

What if we understood that we can teach the important ideas and skills of the disciplines in a hundred different ways? And that students can learn them in a hundred different ways? And that knowledge is loose in the world and should never be circumscribed by lists of standards, texts, and pacing guides?

What if we understood that standards are ingredients for dinner and that real teaching requires us to make dinner with those standards, not serve them cold, singly, and in isolation from the flavors of our students' lives and our own?

What if we were willing to suspend the notions that teacher-focused, batch processing is the best we can do in the 21st century for students whose entry points, cultures, interests, languages, and perspectives quite literally span the globe?

What if we realized that time is far more fluid than we perceive it to be, and that the flexibility of time is one of the teacher's greatest tools for supporting the success of each learner who comes our way?

What if we saw assessment as mentoring student progress rather than judging it? What if we understood formative assessment to be as much an indicator of how we are doing in our classrooms as it is of how a student is doing in our classroom?

What if we insisted on measuring and being accountable for the growth of each learner rather than focusing solely on a century-old system of letters and numbers that, by definition, will be a misfit for too many learners?

And what if we saw *all* our work as ensemble rather than solo? What if, in nearly all planning, decision making, and reflecting, we turned to our students and said, "How should we go about this? How would you like to show what you're learning? How will we know what excellence looks like—for you, and for all of us? What really matters in this work, and what is window dressing? What went wrong yesterday, and how do we repair it? How are we doing as a community? What must each of us do to support the success of all of us?"

And most of all, what if we knew in our core that one of our greatest opportunities and obligations is to feed and teach from our own unique passions, ingenuity, and professional judgment?

This book presents these truths to us directly, clearly, and compellingly. It is rich with voices, illustrations, and classroom examples that model the ideas, mentor our growth, and make it more exciting to say, "Why not" than "Yes, but . . . ."

—**Carol Ann Tomlinson, EdD**

William Clay Parrish, Jr. Professor and Chair
Educational Leadership, Foundations, and Policy
Curry School of Education, University of Virginia

Preface

"I never teach my pupils. I only attempt to provide the conditions in which they can learn."

—(often attributed to) Albert Einstein

Why Did I Write This Book?

When I think of students' boredom in school (and many teachers' reactions to students' boredom), I can't help but recall Bill Watterson's *Calvin and Hobbes* comic, which depicts first a bored and then frustrated Calvin finally belting out "BORRRING!!!" in utter frustration. The next frame shows Calvin muttering, "Yeah, yeah . . . kill the messenger," as he heads to the principal's office (Watterson, 1993). I think of this cartoon to remind myself that I first must engage my students before I can expect them to learn anything, and our students' voices can tell us so much as long as we are willing to listen.

As a student, I loved school. However, even though I liked school, I never quite understood why my day was composed primarily of marathons of boredom aside from a few bursts of time when I was really "engaged" in what I was learning. I often wondered why it was generally acceptable for so many students to find school boring when humans are inherently designed to seek knowledge and to master skills.

I continued to ponder the idea of boredom in school when I became a teacher. During my first year as a teacher, I taught in a fashion similar to how I was taught. I vividly remember one winter afternoon standing at my overhead projector, scribbling notes for my students to copy (to take home and memorize) and thinking to myself, *"This is so boring."*

I knew that students deserved more. If I was bored, my students surely were, too. I also questioned how much my students were *learning* rather than *memorizing*. I knew that if I was going to last in the field of education, I needed to do things differently. I needed to teach in a way that engaged and sustained the interest and attention of *all* my students, while ensuring they were learning.

I quickly learned that the primary contributor to boredom in the classroom was the factory model, one-size-fits-all approach to teaching and learning. The classic markers of "school" (tests, memorization, and homework) needed to be replaced with classic markers of the "real world" (variety of assessments, spaced practice, and a passion that drives you to do work outside of mandated hours).

Now, as a veteran educator, and a mother of two school-aged children, I have an additional impetus for sharing the content of this book.

1. The push for an overhaul of the factory model of education excites me. However, what I often see is simply a shift to the same old (boring, inefficient) methods of teaching with the addition of technology. In a time of educational movements and common district initiatives, many teachers seek guidance as to how to marry movements and mandates. *How can we throw out the textbook and ensure students are learning all the content? How can we promote innovation through our assessments and then assess our students with a standardized test? How can we meet the needs of all our students when they are required to meet the same standards?*

2. I have witnessed the profound impact that using student voice as the driver of instructional decisions has on student success.

There is a way to marry educational trends and mandates while allowing our students' individual and collective voices to permeate our decision-making process. The way to do this is through *student-driven differentiation*.

This book is unlike any other book you have ever seen on differentiation. I will not use the word *differentiation* as often as you may guess a book on differentiation would because, with student-driven differentiation, differentiation is not an afterthought or something else "to do." It's deliberate. It makes sense. It is vital. It embodies the words of John Hattie (2012) in *Visible Learning for Teachers*:

> The key is for teachers to have a clear reason for differentiation, and relate what they do differently. (p. 110)

What Is Student-Driven Differentiation?

Differentiation is traditionally defined as an approach to teaching in which educators actively plan for students' differences so that all students can best learn. In a differentiated classroom, teachers divide their time, resources, and efforts to effectively teach students who have various backgrounds, readiness and skill levels, and interests.

The educational field is lacking tangible information and action plans on how to differentiate for students in today's classroom. The vast majority of literature available on differentiation prescribes methods of differentiation that apply to the factory model of teaching complete with worksheets or traditional lesson plans.

Figure P.1   Student-Driven Differentiation Road Map

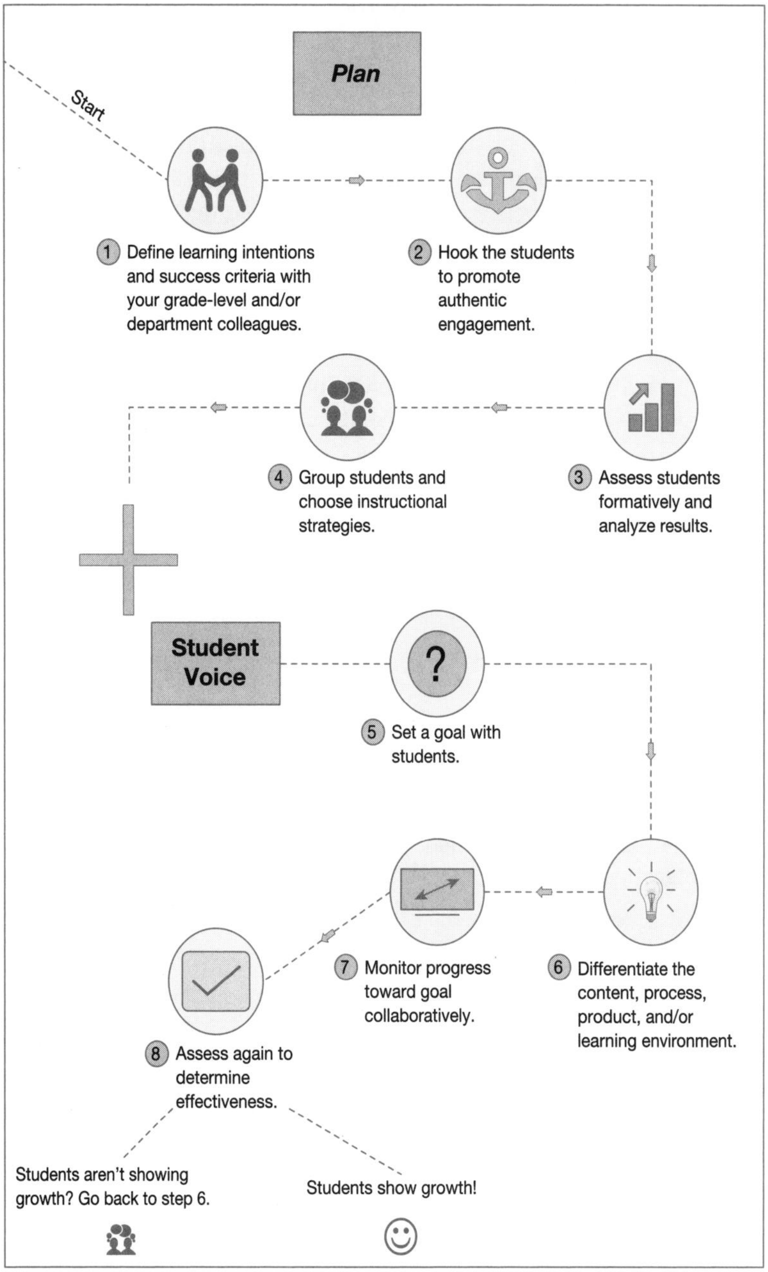

Student-driven differentiation shifts the focus from what students are going to *do* to what students need to *learn*. The focus also shifts from the teacher as the owner of the knowledge and the students as the receivers of such knowledge. Student-driven differentiation requires teachers to find a healthy balance in their relationships with *all* students, use multiple types of evidence to ensure student growth, and partner with students in the process (see Figure P.1).

This method centers on creating learning environments where the students have control over their learning. Differentiation is not an afterthought, nor is it determined without student feedback. Student-driven differentiation shifts teacher planning from "what do I do with these students?" to "what do these students need?"

When differentiating instruction (student driven or not), teachers are mindful that some students will master *content* (what is to be learned) and skills more quickly, while some students will struggle to learn the same content and skills. With student-driven differentiation, rather than plan in advance how to address student needs, students' voices (collective and individual) are sought to craft the plan.

Student-Driven Differentiation

- Shifts the focus from what students are *going to do* to what students *need to learn*
- Requires teachers to find common ground with all students
- Creates learning environments where students have control over their learning
- Gives students the autonomy to create, learn, and grow at their own pace
- Requires honest and mutually respectful teacher–student relationships
- Students' voices (collective and individual) are sought to craft the plan

---

Students' needs are then considered and organically embedded into units that are designed to address the progression of learning standards, while simultaneously giving students autonomy to create, learn, and grow at their pace.

Student-Driven Leadership: A Crucial Component to Student-Driven Differentiation

To ensure a school system (rather than individual teachers) embodies a culture of student-driven differentiation, student-driven leadership is a crucial component. We must not forget that teachers do not teach in isolation; *all stakeholders play a part in the success of our students.* Throughout this book, you will hear the voices of teachers, building administrators, central office administrators, students, and parents. Educational leaders who grant their teachers autonomy and genuinely encourage them to take risks will find that student-driven differentiation will spread throughout their organization organically.

Furthermore, student-driven leadership relies on the hallmarks of traditional differentiation (using formative assessment and making data-informed decisions). However, student-driven leaders allow teachers leeway to figure out, sometimes through trial and error, the best ways to do this and provide them the appropriate supports (including time) to do so. Student-driven leaders seek the voice of their learners *(teachers)* and encourage more teachers to become leaders.

In turn, student-driven teacher leaders focus on positivity, celebrating each other's successes, and collectively building their organization's professional capacity to meet the needs of all students. Lastly, and most importantly, student-driven leaders ensure they either know each student personally, or that all students have teachers who seek to understand them and incorporate their wants and needs into the curriculum, instruction, and assessment.

How to Read This Book

This book is not prescriptive. It has checklists with guiding questions and real examples of how practitioners have been able to weave together the controllable and uncontrollable factors we face as educators and relinquish control of fears that may have subconsciously prevented us from reaching our ultimate goal: the success of all students.

Most importantly, the examples shared in this book are all relevant to the real world. Simply put, students perform better when they are working toward *something*—not a grade, not a bell, but a culminating event, an audience, or building their own efficacy as *they reach their learning goals.* This book will illustrate many examples of authentic learning using student-driven differentiation as the foundation for these experiences.

To aid you in implementing student-driven differentiation in your classroom, we have placed several of the book's resources online for easy access. You can view these resources by visiting the companion website at http://resources.corwin.com/studentdrivendifferentiation.

website

This book is divided into three parts:

Part I: Lays the foundation for student-driven differentiation

Part II: Describes the process of planning and student-driven differentiation

Part III: Motivates and supports you in your student-driven differentiation journey

Before we get started, I offer you a few important pieces of advice, and I insist you remind yourself of these suggestions frequently:

1. The goal of differentiation is to meet the needs of all students. That is your starting point and ending point. There is no "messing up" student-driven differentiation as long as you are constantly asking yourself, "Is this student growing?" And, more importantly, *asking the student,* "What do you need to grow?"

2. Try one thing at a time. Think surgeon over ER doctor: Get really good at one thing, then move on to another. I encourage you to pick the area that interests you most.

3. If it feels like you are trying to stick a square peg in a round hole, you probably are, and that's ok. Just stop. Cut yourself some slack and find a new peg or a new hole.

4. If you are reading this book, you care about students! That is the most important skill to have when incorporating student-driven differentiation into your practice. And guess what—*you* have the highest impact on your students' success. Be proud of yourself!

5. I am not a researcher. I am a practitioner, like you. I have worked diligently to apply the findings of research in a practical way. My goal for this book is to share how I have done this and help you discover ways to use student voice to drive differentiation, too.

Finally, (*spoiler alert*) the best part of reading this book is that, over time, differentiating instruction in this method will ensure you continue to *love* your job. You will be energized when you enter the classroom each morning, and you will go home feeling proud of the learning you facilitated. Most importantly, your students will feel the same way.

Happy reading!

Acknowledgments

Writing acknowledgments for this book is quite the undertaking for me. I am incredibly grateful for the many people who contributed to this book in one way or another: my students, my colleagues (past and present), my family, and my fellow educators. There are a few people, however, that I want to thank specifically, because without them, I could not have written this book.

▶ Keith, Keller, Mallory, Mom, Dad, Nannie, Paula, Brad, Paige, Brielle, Halie, Neal, Michelle, Cece, Alice, Debbie, Gary, Dean, Adrianna, Abby, Stephen, Jamarion, Jaylen, Dana, Carin, and Nikki—thank you for your unwavering support.

▶ Chris Hull, thank you for giving me my wings and the support I need to fly.

▶ Peter DeWitt, thank you for taking a chance on me and for guiding me down what has proven to be a most amazing path. You have immeasurably impacted my life, and I am eternally grateful.

▶ Carol Ann Tomlinson, thank you for being my first teacher on differentiation and for continuing to mentor me. You are and always have been an incredible inspiration. You help all educators keep it real. Thank you.

▶ Mike Andriulli, thank you for the daily pep talks, sharing your pragmatic problem-solving approach, and for being a constant reminder of all the good that exists in the field of education.

▶ George Couros, thank you for always telling me like it is and then telling me again. I appreciate and value your candor and insight.

▶ To my Oliver McCracken Middle School Family (many of whom have contributed to this book), thank you for being my partners and cheerleaders. Your encouragement and your remarkable dedication to the field of education continue to inspire me.

▶ To my fellow educators turned friends: Becky Fischer, Dane Delli, Renee Fitzsimmons, Pete Helfers, Jen Marten, Samantha Mason, Mark McCord, Mike Taglia, Zach Peterson, Corey Tafoya, and Robert Ward—thank you for your sharing your expertise, time, and for just being you.

▶ To my former students: Josie Adamson, Daniel Meyer, Julia Mkrtychian, and Stephanie Sordini—thank you for your candid contributions to this book. Your voices will help educators and students understand differentiation from a different point of view.

▶ Ariel Bartlett Curry, Desirée Bartlett, Jessica Vidal, Lana Arndt, and Amy Schroller at Corwin. As I have said many times, I wish you could follow me everywhere. Your guidance, patience, and positivity have been invaluable. Thank you!

▶ Corwin, thank you for the opportunity. I am honored to be a part of your organization.

About the Author

Lisa Westman has over 15 years of experience as a teacher (gifted humanities, English Language Arts, social studies), and as an instructional coach specializing in differentiation. Lisa is currently a writer, consultant, and speaker, working with school systems across the country to effectively implement student-driven differentiation, standards-based learning, and instructional coaching programs. Lisa is passionate about teaching and learning; she is dedicated to effecting change which positively impacts both student and educator learning.

Lisa frequently presents for school districts and at educational conferences. She has presented at ASCD, Visible Learning, Illinois Association for Gifted Children, Illinois Computing Educators, Illinois Education and Technology Conference, and Illinois Council of Instructional Coaching. Lisa is a frequent opinion contributor to *EdWeek, EdWeek Teacher,* Corwin Connect, and her personal blog, Put Me In, Coach. This is her first book.

Lisa is married to an educator, is the parent of a third-grader and a sixth-grader, enjoys destressing at the Bar Method, and loves music and the City of Chicago!

To Keith, Keller, Mallory, and Darci:
the best teachers I have ever had, by far.
I love you.

Part I
Foundation

Relationships Come First

What Are the Criteria for Positive Teacher–Student Relationships?

Figure 1.1   Three Tenets of Forming Genuine Relationships With Students

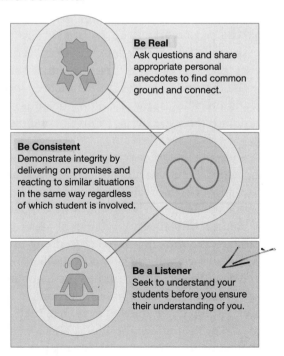

Be Real
Ask questions and share appropriate personal anecdotes to find common ground and connect.

Be Consistent
Demonstrate integrity by delivering on promises and reacting to similar situations in the same way regardless of which student is involved.

Be a Listener
Seek to understand your students before you ensure their understanding of you.

"The single biggest problem in communication is the illusion that it has taken place."

—George Bernard Shaw

Dr. Russell Quaglia and his team at the Quaglia Institute for Student Aspirations have spent years collecting and analyzing data about how all education stakeholders feel about their educational experience. Quaglia's 2016 National Student Voice report discloses a statistic that is, simply put, shocking. After surveying over 38,000 students in Grades 6–12, the researchers found that only 58% of students feel like their teachers respect them, while 99% of teachers report that they respect their students (Quaglia, 2016).

The discrepancy between these numbers is alarming, but not surprising. This is due in large part to how we (1) define respect between teachers and students and (2) the steps we take to develop respectful relationships with students. While many teachers feel relationships are respectful because students are courteous to them, students don't feel the same because their voice is not heard. A respectful relationship requires both parties to feel equal in their participation. To create a **learning environment** where embedded **differentiation** is effective, respectful relationships are the most crucial piece. They are the foundation on which success sits.

Considering that **student-driven differentiation** relies on students' voices (collective and individual) to determine instruction through strategies like **goal setting** and **feedback**, an **authentic** relationship in which *both parties* are respectful and *feel respected* is essential. Here is the caveat in this statement: If a teacher does not feel respected by a student, it is likely that the student does not feel respected by the teacher. Since the teacher is the professional and the adult in the situation, the onus is on the teacher to create the conditions for respectful relationships and mend any damage previously done.

As I mentioned in the Preface, having children of my own has shaped my professional practice. As luck would have it, my husband (also an educator) and I have had more than our fair share of firsthand experience watching the impact of student–teacher relationships with our oldest child, Keller.

Keller is the student who educators commonly refer to as "that kid." From the moment he was born, our son has been strong-willed and inquisitive, and he likes to push the limits (we have no idea where he gets this from).

Teachers often describe our son as "spirited" or "rambunctious," and he frequently gets in "trouble" at school. In fact, our son got in trouble in his very first classroom setting: the hospital nursery. Yep, that's right. Our newborn was "kicked-out" by the nurse of the nursery after a brief 45-minute stay because he was bothering the other babies by crying too loudly. Needless to say, Keller, who is now in sixth grade, has had some great years at school and some *not so great years* at school. The determining factor in whether our son has a "good" year or "bad" year (as further supported by his **growth** on informal and formal **assessments**) is largely the relationship he has had with his teacher that year.

Although it seems like forming genuine relationships with students is a simple task, unfortunately, as indicated by Quaglia's research, teachers often overestimate how their students feel about their relationships. Teacher–student relationships built on trust and focused on learning can successfully use student voice to exponentially increase achievement. However, those relationships that are based in compliance do not have the same success, and students struggle to learn and grow in this classroom. Often, they struggle in silence unbeknownst to the teacher. One example of this comes from student Josie Adamson, who has **selective mutism**. Josie, who recently completed her sophomore year in high school, shares a little bit about how relationships with her teachers have impacted her learning.

> **Selective mutism:** Selective mutism usually begins during childhood. A child with selective mutism does not speak in certain situations, like at school. Children with selective mutism may also show social anxiety disorder, excessive shyness, fear of social embarrassment, and/or social isolation and withdrawal (American Speech Language Hearing Association, 2017).

Student Voice

Josie Adamson, High School Junior

Skokie, IL

Student–teacher relationships have always been very important to me because I have selective mutism, which is a fear of talking, and the teachers who have welcomed me with open arms without trying to change me are the teachers I remember most.

These relationships have helped me as a student because they make me feel valued for who I am right now. I have found that the classes where my teachers do this are the ones where I usually put in the most effort and get the best grades. I have also noticed that the teachers who do care have continued to be a part of my life for years after I left their class.

While I have had many great relationships with my teachers, there are definitely a couple that have had the strongest impact on me. My first super-strong relationship with a teacher that I really remember was in third grade, and it started the first time I met her. I was starting a few days into the year because I had just gotten home from a trip, so I had to lug my supplies with me after everyone else had done it days before, and my teacher came up to me and asked if I needed help carrying it. It was something so

(Continued)

(Continued)

little, but it got rid of all the anxiety I had for starting late, and she continued to watch out for me and helped to find ways for me to participate in activities where I was supposed to speak. For one project, we had to present at round up for all the parents, and my teacher knew I couldn't do that but she still wanted it presented.

My strongest relationship with a teacher was when I was in seventh grade; she was my social studies and honors English teacher. I knew from the first day of class that she was someone I could trust, she was very open and kind and, over the year, got to know all of us very well and truly cared about each of us as individuals and knew what everyone's strengths and weaknesses were. She tried to help each of us focus on our strengths, while also addressing our areas for growth. She never tried to change me, yet she has helped me so much with working toward talking and has always been there for me even when we disagree on a subject.

While I have had many good relationships with teachers, I have also had a handful of bad relationships with teachers because they tried to change who I was rather than learning what they could do to help me be successful with who I already was. My first experience with a teacher who tried to change who I was instead of getting to know me was in elementary school, and my teacher spent the whole year trying to get me to talk even after she was informed that she wouldn't be able to do so. This left me constantly on edge and scared to go to school, and this also led to a strong disconnect between the two of us leaving me miserable because it felt like my teacher hated me and I didn't know why. It wasn't until I started middle school that I realized that maybe she didn't hate me and was just trying to change me; I can be around her now and am fine. But, I wonder what that year would have been like if things were different."

How Do You Build Respectful Relationships?

With Josie's story in mind, an obvious first step to including student voice is to simply ask students, "How do you feel about learning in this classroom?" on a frequent basis. But, before you can ask this question and start including student voice as a measure to determine how to differentiate, you must create a classroom community that is equally supportive and respectful of all members. Constructing this environment starts with building authentic relationships with students (see Figure 1.1). Teachers can accomplish this by remembering to always

▶ Be *real*

▶ Be *consistent*

▶ Be a *listener*

When teachers model these qualities, students will overwhelmingly respond similarly. This environment allows students to take risks, celebrate each other's strengths, and promote organic collaboration. Some of the biggest "differentiation killers" like top-down classroom management or the perception of not being "fair" do not come into play when relationships are built on these tenets. However, to be clear, this is not to say that teachers and students are *friends*. There is still a clear distinction of the roles of teacher and student; however, the respect shown for these roles is founded in genuine respect rather than being a result of compliance measures.

Tenet 1: Be Real

Have you ever run into a student outside of school? Perhaps you bumped into a student and his mom as you turned the corner at the grocery store. Or, worse, you look up from slathering sunscreen on yourself or your own children at the public pool to see your former student peeking at you from behind the water slide?

If you have experienced something similar, you may have felt uncomfortable when you made eye contact with your student, and you may have sensed that your level of uncomfortableness was nothing compared to theirs. It's as if students are shocked when they realize that *teachers have real lives, too.*

And, we sure do. We have families, hobbies, interests, fears, and have been faced with substantially more life-changing (for good or bad) experiences than the majority of our students.

Yet, often times, it can be difficult for teachers to tap into these personal experiences and use them to find common ground and connect with students. There is a fine line between letting your guard down and oversharing. But, it is right on this line where the magic happens.

And, counterintuitive to what logic tells us, the best time to find common ground is when students are off-task. Off-task behavior is not a problem; it is an opportunity to build relationships with students and simultaneously gather information to potentially help inform how to differentiate the **content** or **process** of the learning activity for that student.

> The best time to find common ground is when students are off-task. . . . When teachers engage with off-task behaviors rather than try to shut them down, they are more successful at redirecting students and also form bonds instead of barriers with them.

As an instructional coach, I had had the opportunity to see how many teachers respond to off-task behavior. I found that when teachers engage with off-task behaviors rather than try to shut it down, they are more successful at redirecting students and also form bonds instead of barriers with them.

For example, as I was co-teaching a lesson with a teacher, we noticed a group of students were socializing about a football game, which had nothing to do with the task at hand. The teacher did not become bothered with this behavior and let the group engage for a bit. Then, she walked over to the group and said, "I'm so sorry for eavesdropping, but I overheard you discussing the Packers game and I have to say, that even though my father would be heartbroken if he heard this (he won't even eat cheese during football season), I was happy the Packers won."

The teacher and students then proceeded to engage in a brief conversation about football and then after a couple of minutes the teacher said, "Oh my gosh, I am so sorry. I have gotten your group completely off-task. Where were you all? Let's see how I can help you get up to speed." I was amazed to see how quickly the students got back on track and were candid about their stumbling blocks with the assignment that likely contributed to the off-task behavior. With just a few minutes of time lost, the teacher was able to provide **feedback** to the students to get them on track, while noting that football was an interest for some members in this group.

> **Feedback:** Information given to students connected to learning goals, which provides insight as to where they are and where they need to go next.

Now, it is important to note that there are times when student off-task behavior or comments are profoundly disrespectful (typically comments that are racist, sexist, or that alienate others), and these comments must be addressed in a different way, but the key here is consistency in how these instances are handled, and I elaborate more on this in the next section on Tenet 2 of building successful relationships.

Being real with students is also critical when students are experiencing a profound change in their lives (death in the family, divorce, eviction, etc.) or a chronic struggle (learning difference, negative feeling toward self, etc.). How teachers respond to students during this time can either build up or shut down relationships with students—both those directly affected and their classmates.

In these situations, teachers often feel the need to make things right for these students or, conversely, pretend like the situation doesn't exist so the student doesn't get upset. But, sometimes, teachers can't make things right, and not acknowledging a situation doesn't make it go away; it just makes students feel isolated.

Therefore, I have found that teachers who have the strongest relationships with students find that middle ground. They acknowledge the student's feelings without offering a fix: "*I can imagine this is a confusing time for you now. I am so sorry you have to deal with this. I wanted you to know that while I can't understand (unless you have had the same situation) your exact circumstances, I have experienced (loss, fear of the unknown, etc.), and it was helpful for me to know other people understood I was experiencing a range of feelings."*

During a time of stress, sharing just the right amount of information about yourself helps students see you as vulnerable, honest, and minimally just interesting. When we plan differentiated lessons for our students, we want them to demonstrate these exact qualities. Genuinely modeling these traits is the most effective way to elicit these responses from our students.

Tenet 2: Be Consistent

The online English Oxford dictionary defines *consistent* as "acting or done in the same way over time, especially so as to be fair or accurate." Being consistent goes hand in hand with being real. Educators have the autonomy to determine how we want to handle behavior issues, academic concerns, and day-to-day procedures; simply make a determination to handle these issues consistently over time and from student to student. Acknowledge that we all have a natural tendency to react differently to similar situations depending on which student(s) are involved and take action steps to overcome that lack of consistency.

All humans have underlying **biases**, but we may not be aware of them. Author and speaker, Tonya Ward Singer, who has studied implicit bias states "everyone has implicit bias and implicit associations don't always align with our intentional beliefs. For example, a teacher may believe all races are equal, and also may unconsciously associate Latino students with low achievement" (Singer, 2015).

One of the most profound examples of implicit bias was written about by Brian Crooks in July 2016 in a Facebook post that went viral. Crooks's example resonated so strongly on social media that parts of the post were later picked up by the Chicago Tribune and published in the article, "What It's Like to Be Black in Naperville, America" in July of 2016. To understand the article, it might help to know that Naperville, Illinois, is a predominantly white, affluent suburb, about 30 miles west of Chicago. Specifically, Crooks recalls being elated to be part of the gifted program in his elementary school. When he was in third grade, Crooks describes a group work experience he had which still resonates with him today as an adult as a strong example of microaggressions:

> —we had to give a short speech about something we'd learned during the year. All of the groups broke off to divvy up the work when my teacher came over to my group. Wouldn't it be "easier" and more fun for me if my group did our presentation as a rap? I'm eight years old. I have no history writing any kind of music, much less a full

3 or 4 minutes of rap verses for me and my teammates. But, I tried. The other kids just expected it to be natural for me. They looked at me like, "What do you mean you don't know how to rap?" We ended up just doing it as a regular presentation like everybody else, and afterward my teacher came up to me and said, "I thought you guys were going to rap? I was looking forward to MC Brian."

As Brian goes on to explain, he fully realizes that his teacher did not know she was making a racially-insensitive statement. But, then again, he asks, "why would she? It's not like she'd had deep conversation about how Black people feel about their Blackness, or the way Black people internalized the way White people feel about our Blackness."

As this recollection by Crooks illustrates, even when our actions are well-intended, we often allow biases to interfere with forming mutually respectful relationships. This teacher assumed things about the student that she thought were allowing her to differentiate for his interests. But, she didn't actually talk with the student and get input from him. To let student voice drive differentiation, we cannot make assumptions.

Instead, we must recognize our biases and then take actions to overcome them and form meaningful relationships with all students. One way to do this is by applying the method Verna Myers (2014) discusses in her Ted Talk "How to Overcome Our Biases: Walk Boldly Toward Them."

1. Accept that you have biases.

2. Look for examples that contradict your bias.

3. Engage with someone from that (gender, ethnicity, age, etc.) in a way that is more respectful and that doesn't act on your previously held bias.

Tip: Keep a class list handy at all times (on paper or digital) and mark each time you celebrate the strength of a student to make sure you celebrate students equitably.

Then, keep track of how many times they celebrate each other.

Once we acknowledge our biases and resolve to confront them, it might be helpful to try out approaches such as positive behavior intervention systems (PBIS) and programs like Sprick and Baldwin's (2009) *CHAMPs: A Positive & Proactive Approach to Classroom Management.*

Remember that student-driven differentiation focuses on students' strengths, never their deficits. Take time to celebrate what makes students unique and special about a student and how that skill or quality can benefit a group, an individual, and you as the teacher. Celebrate students consistently (over time and from student to student).

Tenet 3: Be a Listener

This is perhaps the hardest quality to consistently demonstrate. This is because our natural inclination is to *not* listen, especially to children, for a variety of reasons, which I elaborated on in my October 2016 blogpost.

Actually, I Wasn't Listening to Anything You Said

by Lisa Westman

October 4, 2016

Finding Common Ground blogs.edweek.org

> *"Preschool children, on average, ask their parents about 100 questions a day. Why, why, why—sometimes parents just wish it'd stop. Tragically, it does stop. By middle school they've pretty much stopped asking."* Po Bronson and Ashley Merryman, *The Creativity Crisis*, Newsweek

> *"I didn't do my homework last night."*

> *"I think our house is haunted; has anyone ever died here?"*

> *"I cannot find my keys."*

These were three comments made by my children just this morning (ok, one was from my husband). And, these were three bids for attention from my family that I did not acknowledge appropriately. I reprimanded my son, diminished my daughter's annual autumn fear of ghosts, and I ignored my husband. Until recently, I wouldn't have given my responses a second thought. My family spoke, I responded appropriately. Therefore, I was listening to them. However, this wouldn't be accurate or fair to them. I heard the words they said, but I wasn't listening.

I could make an excuse and say, *"family is different. I don't need to use the same listening skills with them that I try to use with colleagues,"* but, the truth is, good listening is a full-time job. We can't turn it off and on again. I made this realization last spring after attending Jim Knight's Better Conversations workshop and reading his book by the same title. Knight suggests that we aren't always objective self-evaluators. He writes:

> *"One way to improve conversations is to identify what we really want to believe about how we interact with others. We are not slaves to our beliefs. We get to choose them, but to do so, we must surface our current beliefs and then consider what alternative beliefs might better describe who we are and who we want to be."*

(Continued)

(Continued)

My belief was that I was a good listener. I actively listened to what others were saying, let them drive the conversation, and responded accordingly. In an effort to confirm my beliefs, I filmed myself facilitating a roundtable discussion with other instructional coaches, and I was shocked when I watched the footage. I saw myself falling prey to some of the biggest listening predators: interrupting, asking questions from my point-of-view, and offering solutions disguised as questions.

Why did I do this?

Stephen Covey, the author of *7 Habits of Highly Effective People* (2016), says that highly effective listeners:

"Seek first to understand, then to be understood."

Covey explains, however, that the majority of people do just the opposite. They seek first to be understood, to get their point across. Most people prepare answers without actually listening to their conversation partner because they listen autobiographically. When people listen in this way, they typically respond in one of four ways: by judging (speaker is right or wrong), by probing (asking questions from their point-of-view), by offering solutions, or by analyzing based on their personal experiences.

I realized I had spent years listening autobiographically. I had also spent years thinking that this was an effective way of listening. I also realized that, sadly, I had also probably spent years listening autobiographically to my students. To me, this was the biggest shame.

Educators have the unique opportunity to shape the next generation of adult listeners by modeling effective listening with their current students. Teachers and administrators (including me) often claim we encourage students to advocate for themselves. But, the question is: When students advocate for themselves are we actually listening?

I would venture to say that surely some educators are listening, but, on the whole, we have room for improvement. Simply put, listening with the intent to understand can be even harder to do with children than with adults because of inherent differences in life experience and status. Therefore, adults may unproductively listen to children in one of the following ways:

- With superiority: The teacher is in charge. The teacher needs to be understood before the students can express their thoughts.

- By being defensive: Students comments and questions (why do we have to learn this?) may feel like an attack. Therefore, we stop listening to what students are saying to prepare our rebuttal.

- By presuming: We assume we know what or why a student is saying something without asking clarifying questions to truly understand why.

recommended Book (handwritten annotation)

> ▶ By not being present: The timing of questions and comments from students may not be ideal, only increasing our urge to prepare answers without fully listening.
>
> Due to such listening blocks, many students' attempts to advocate for themselves fall on deaf ears. Even though educators may not intend to listen inattentively, the results are the same. Students will eventually stop trying to engage us in conversation, and we are perpetuating the use of ineffective listening.
>
> What can we do to become better listeners?
>
> We can make a concerted effort to be better listeners to anyone with whom we engage in conversation: adult or child. We will likely find that our students learn more, we will learn more, and our students will have more productive conversations with each other. If we can suspend judgment, let go of status, and really listen, we undoubtedly will be better able to meet the needs of all students. The biggest success, however, will likely be that our students will grow up to be more effective adult listeners.

listening

Successful implementation of student-driven differentiation ultimately relies on truly listening to what our students say. Although, there are certain times and certain students that may test our listening resolve, listening and considering what our students tell us is a non-negotiable.

There are still times a student will say, "I don't care about this" or "I don't want to learn anything." And, as tempting as it would be to pull the authority card, we need to look at these challenges as our greatest opportunity to put the student in the driver's seat.

Discussion Questions

▶ How will you model being real and being consistent? → *see the student's problems understand the situation*

▶ What steps will you take to ensure you are really listening to students? *Let go of status. Really listen, suspend judgment*

▶ How will you discover, confront, and tame your implicit biases? *Ht someone accept you have biases, engage known with from authority community*

▶ What are your feelings about mutually respectful relationships between students and teachers?

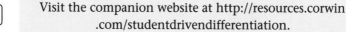

Visit the companion website at http://resources.corwin .com/studentdrivendifferentiation.

Chapter 2

Differentiation Is What Happens When Teachers Focus on Student Growth

The year 2001 was my first year as a teacher. It was one of the best and worst years of my career. It was also the year I started to differentiate for my students. I didn't differentiate instruction for my students to comply with my district's strategic plan. I hadn't (yet) read about differentiation in a book, and I certainly hadn't been taught in differentiated classrooms as a student. Rather, I had an experience that was so emotionally compelling that I saw no other option but to differentiate for my students.

At the time, I taught seventh- and eighth-grade gifted humanities in a small suburban community just north of Chicago. The teacher who held this role previously, Dawn, had been promoted to Director of Engaged Learning for the district. In her new role, Dawn was to work with *all* teachers (veteran and new) on their instruction. Dawn was beloved by students, parents, teachers, and administrators. She was a living legend—her face is literally memorialized in bronze on a plaque outside of the district office . . . next to the street named in her honor.

I, on the other hand, like most 22-year-olds, thought I already knew everything. I mean, I had a lot of educational experience. I had just completed 17 years of school as student and was still taking grad school classes. I knew what to do. I would teach my students the way I was taught. My students were high-achievers, so I simply gave them "harder" and "longer" assignments. And, for a few months, all seemed to be going just fine.

November came, and I experienced my first parent–teacher conferences. I spent extra time preparing to meet with the parents of a student who I believed was not putting forth any effort. Frankly, I had no idea why Joey (not his real name) was in the gifted class. I remember sitting across from the parents of this seventh-grade boy and telling them that their son could benefit from putting forth more effort, completing his homework, and being more respectful to his classmates and me.

I expected the parents to apologize on behalf of their son. I expected them to feel embarrassed by his performance. But, this is not what happened. Instead, the parents started asking me questions like: "Is it possible that Joey isn't completing homework because the homework is not useful? Do you think that Joey would be more respectful to you if you were more respectful of his needs?" As I stumbled over my answers trying desperately to defend my professional actions and authority, the father of this child interrupted me and said,

> "You have some big shoes to fill, and from the looks of it, you will never be able to fill them."

Ouch! What a blow to my ego and a test of my emotions. I bit the inside of my cheeks so as to not break down in front of them. Finally, the conference ended. But, my journey was just beginning . . . *what was I going to do now?*

Luckily for me, conferences directly preceded a 5-day Thanksgiving break. During that break, I spent 2 days sulking, 2 days being angrily defensive, and on the 5th day, something changed. I asked myself:

> "Could these parents be right?"

Perhaps the homework I assigned was irrelevant. Come to think of it . . . I hadn't ever thought about students' learning needs; I was simply focused on covering content. Then it hit me.

> "Maybe, just maybe, I was the one who needed to change and not the student."

This was a very scary realization. I had absolutely no idea what this change would look like or where to start. I knew I wanted to teach in a way that would best meet the academic and social-emotional needs of each of my students, but how in the world would I do this? Plus, what if the other parents didn't agree with my new approach? What if they were upset that I was no longer going to give homework for the sake of giving homework? What if they were upset that their child was assessed using a different method than one of his classmates?

The following Monday, I arrived at school early and found Dawn (my predecessor). I told Dawn everything that happened at conferences. I rallied off all of my fears and questions. Dawn acknowledged my concerns and said:

> "These are the experiences that mold us as educators. You can choose to try something new, or you can continue doing what you are doing and see what happens."

I chose to try something new. This was the best decision I ever made. Dawn partnered with me to ensure that I was able to meet all of my students' needs. Our work together largely centered on our joint learning from another legend, differentiation expert Carol Ann Tomlinson. Tomlinson's book, *The Differentiated Classroom* (2014), became our bible.

Differentiation Lessons Learned

The year 2001 was the start of my path to learn how to best differentiate for my students, and even as a differentiation instructional coach and consultant, I am *still* learning more about the how and why of differentiation. What helps me the most in my work with differentiation is to remember the following five lessons I have learned and keep them in the forefront of my mind as I plan instruction or work with others to plan instruction.

Lesson 1: Differentiation Is Not a Goal—It Is a Result

Contrary to popular belief, differentiation is not something else teachers "have to do." Rather, differentiation is what happens when teachers' focus is student growth. In fact, differentiation is the natural byproduct of correct implementation of almost all research-based, high-impact instructional strategies. *In short, differentiation is not the goal: It is the result.*

Take for example the samples of teacher goals in Figure 2.1, one goal in each category of **the Big Four**

The "Big Four" (classroom management, content, instruction, and formative assessment) is a framework for improving instruction (Knight, 2007, p. 141).

(classroom management, content, instruction, **formative assessment**) set by teachers during instructional coaching cycles (these goals are applicable to teachers who work with a coach or who work with teammates or administrators to achieve professional goals) (Knight, 2007, p. 141). You can see that while all of these goals resulted in differentiation, none of the teachers had the word differentiation in their stated goal.

Differentiation is what happens when teachers' focus is student growth.

Figure 2.1   Professional Goals Resulting in Differentiation

Classroom Management

Goal: I want to decrease the number of disruptions.

- *Data collected:* Number of disruptions in a 40-minute period
- *Strategy used:* Break up whole group instruction with structured partner work
- *How did differentiation ensue?* Rally Coach allowed for students at different places in their learning to partner and be challenged appropriately

Content

Goal: I want students to see the relevancy of the content in a unit.

- *Data collected:* Student engagement data
- *Strategy used:* Essential question(s)
- *How did differentiation ensue?* Students self-identified areas of relevance to the content and then wrote pieces on different topics all related to the subject area, rather than in previous years where all students wrote on the same topic.

Instruction

Goal: I want to engage more students in class discussions.

- *Data collected:* Types, kind, level of questions asked and number of students volunteering to answer
- *Strategy used:* Questioning (using Bloom's taxonomy and Webb's Depth of Knowledge) and options for multiple students to answer simultaneously (using various tech tools)
- *How did differentiation ensue?* Asking questions at various levels (more open than closed questions, more analysis questions than knowledge questions) increased the number of students contributing answers that allowed the teacher to assess students' understanding of concepts more thoroughly and adjust pacing for those students (differentiate the process) accordingly.

Formative Assessment
Goal: I want to involve students in the formative assessment process.

- *Data Collected:* Type of peer feedback offered

- *Strategy used:* Peer feedback and video analysis of feedback

- *How did differentiation ensue?* Student products were differentiated as peer feedback promoted student autonomy and allowed choice in showing mastery of a concept or skill.

Goals aligned to The Big Four Framework outlined by Jim Knight in *Instructional Coaching* (2007).

Lesson 2: The Terms *Data* and *Assessment* Are Often Misunderstood

I was never the best geometry student, but the one thing that stuck with me was "all squares are rectangles, but not all rectangles are squares." The same can be said about assessments, "all tests are assessments, but not all assessments are tests."

The *Merriam-Webster's Dictionary* defines the word *assess* as, "to make an approximate or tentative judgment." Tests can certainly do this. However, often times, tests are the least effective way to ascertain where students are and what they need. Test results amass a certain type of information, and to differentiate successfully, other evaluations (observations, writing samples, conversations) and facets (social-emotional, aptitude, growth) of student performance must be considered.

The way we assess and the assessments we utilize give us the data we need to properly differentiate instruction for students.

Figure 2.2   Differentiation: Cleaning a Few Things Up

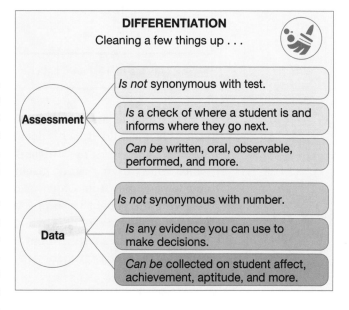

Assessment: method used to determine where a student is in his or her learning

Therefore, we must use a variety of reliable assessments or our attempts to differentiate instruction may fall flat because the assessment data we try to use do not give us the information we need.

The unfortunate thing is that the word *data* does not have a warm connotation. Saying "data" in conjunction with student learning often feels sterile and uncaring. I often hear sentiments like, "students are more than a number."

At the 2016 National ASCD Conference, I had the once-in-a-lifetime opportunity to present on differentiation with differentiation's foremost thought-leader, Carol Ann Tomlinson and interestingly, even Carol Ann sometimes cringes at the word data. I will always remember her response to one participant when he asked a question about using data. Carol Ann said, "Data sounds like something spit out by a machine."

I agree, students are more than a data point. They are more than a number spit out by a machine. So are data themselves. Data are more than just numbers, and they can be gathered and appraised in compassionate ways.

Students are more than a data point.

Let's look at an analogous situation: a child's visit to his pediatrician. When a child visits his doctor, he is more than a number there, too. To form a diagnosis, pediatricians look at a variety of evidence, some of which comes from a lab or machine (weight, temperature, blood count), and some comes from other assessments (conversations, questionnaires, observing the patient perform a task). Yet, there is little complaint about using multiple types of data in a medical setting. In fact, I surmise that if a doctor made a diagnosis without various types of data, gathered through a variety of types of assessment data, there would be quite a bit of protesting by parents.

So, what is the difference? In education, we seem to think the only usable *data* we have are numbers: test scores, IQ scores, attendance rates, etc. This is like saying the only data a doctor can use is the patient's height, weight, blood pressure, etc.

If this were the case, think of how many misdiagnoses would be made from only using these pieces of evidence? The doctor would not have some of the vital information (data) he needs to diagnose the patient and prescribe a course of action.

Instead, doctors are also highly dependent on information that comes directly from the patient via conversations and observations. These are data that are collected with sensitivity and not calculated by an algorithm. Doctors use information from all of these sources to differentiate their approach for their patients, so they thrive.

The same holds true for using data to differentiate for our students in the classroom. When we say the word *data* in education, we are simply referring to the different types of evidence we gather and consider to differentiate instruction for our students, so they thrive.

Lesson 3: It Is Easy to See Different— It Is Not Easy to See Differentiation

This is because in order for something to qualify as differentiation, evidence (qualitative and quantitative) must be considered.

One of the most common questions I get asked is, "What if my principal does a walkthrough? How will they *see* I am differentiating?" The answer is, they won't unless they collect some evidence from speaking with you or speaking with your students. Students could feasibly be working on different tasks in a classroom, but without some probing questions, it can be difficult to ascertain whether or not the tasks have been differentiated and even more difficult to ascertain whether or not the tasks have been differentiated appropriately.

School principals, like 2016 Principal of The Year Mark McCord, are keenly interested in whether or not differentiation is occurring in a classroom because they want to support teachers in their efforts to differentiate, not play a game of "Gotcha." Mark describes his experience observing teachers and looking for differentiation in the vignette below:

Administrator's Voice

Mark McCord, Principal

Stockdick Junior High

Katy, TX

As principal of a Title I eligible campus, I fully recognize the extreme variability in our learners. One critical element to engage our students and lead them

(Continued)

(Continued)

down the path to success is differentiation. When I observe teachers (both formally and informally), I look for certain elements to determine whether or not learning is differentiated appropriately for our students. Let's explore two different language arts classrooms with different levels of differentiation occurring.

Let me start with an undifferentiated eighth-grade lesson I observed. When I entered the room, I noticed that every student had a copy of *Monster*, written by Walter Myers. Booming from a CD player at the front of the room was an audio version of the book with voice actors speaking their parts. I looked to the board for the posted activities. The only thing listed was "Audio Play of *Monster.*" During my time in the class, the teacher stopped the audio two times to ask low-level, clarifying questions. The students were compliant in following along in their books as the audio progressed. Their yawns and slumped posture were all signs that many had tuned out and were not cognitively engaged. I did not question students about their learning because of the whole class nature of the lesson. It felt like this lesson was being done *to* the students instead of *for* the students. I found myself struggling to stay in the room for the full 15 minutes.

In contrast to the eighth-grade lesson was a seventh-grade lesson in which the teacher was employing a Reader's Workshop approach. The first thing I noticed upon entering the room was that a proficiency scale was displayed on the multimedia board at the front. This learning continuum clearly identified the targets along with the scaffolding of skills necessary to show or exceed mastery. I noticed that every student had a different text. Some students were reading or writing independently, while others were working together. The teacher was quietly conferring with a student. I started asking students about their learning. I was impressed that each one of them could identify their level of proficiency based upon the projected scale. Most were working on moving from emerging to proficient. When I asked students who were already proficient how they pushed themselves to exemplary, they pointed to an anchor chart posted in the room. They shared that they were able to create a variety of self-selected products to demonstrate that they were exemplary.

I then moved to eavesdrop on the conferring conversation that

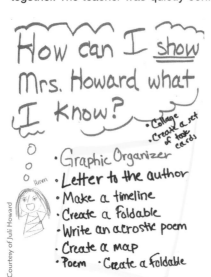

How can I show Mrs. Howard what I know?

• Collage
• Create a set of task cards
• Graphic Organizer
• Letter to the author
• Make a timeline
• Create a foldable
• Write an acrostic poem
• Create a map
• Poem • Create a foldable

Courtesy of Juli Howard

the teacher was having with a student. She was questioning him about characters in his self-selected book. He shared different examples of internal and external character responses. She left him with the charge of looking for connections between character responses and the book's plot. She then made some notes and went to the next student. In this classroom, it was obvious that the teacher was not only differentiating by choice, but also according to their readiness. Students owned their learning in this classroom. Before I knew it, 20 minutes had passed, and I reluctantly left to explore another class.

These two examples are at the opposite ends of the differentiation continuum. I often find it much easier to see when differentiation is not happening than when it is. If, as an administrator, you find yourself in this situation, remember to talk to the students during your time in the classroom. If as a teacher you sometimes struggle to determine the best way to differentiate for your students, again, talk with them. One can never go wrong seeking their students' voices.

Mark's advice to seek student's voice (individually or collectively) to determine how to differentiate for students will produce desirable results for teachers and likewise for administrator's during a walkthrough or observation. If administrators seek to determine whether or not differentiation is occurring in the classroom, they can consider asking students questions such the following, which slightly differ from questions typically asked of students during a walkthrough.

Lesson 4: Differentiation May Never Feel "Easy"

There has rarely been a time where I have thought to myself, "I am doing an amazing job differentiating for my students." As an instructional coach,

Figure 2.3   Questions to Ask on a Differentiation Walkthrough

Ask Students This Question	Instead of This One . . .
What is your learning goal?	What is the learning/lesson objective?
Where are you on your path to reach your goal? How have you been monitoring your success?	What are you working on?
Can you tell me about the roles your groupmates and you have?	What is your group doing?

I interact with dedicated, hardworking teachers who share heartfelt sentiments that they feel stressed because they aren't sure if they are doing a "good job" differentiating instruction. Teachers in this position, like Stephanie Sordini (who happens to be one of my former students and is now a fifth-grade teacher) tend to have a fight-or-flight reaction to differentiation as she describes below:

Teacher Voice

Stephanie Sordini, Fifth-Grade Teacher

Hawthorn School District 73

Lake Zurich, IL

The excitement on the first day of school encompasses so many emotions, not only for students, but for educators as well. The moments of meeting your students on the first day, and only getting a glimpse of their evolving personalities, ambitions, and what sometimes feels like never-ending needs, can be the most exciting, while equally exhausting day. The truth behind the first bell can be some of the most rewarding truths, accompanied by many unspoken struggles. Differentiation is one of those rewarding struggles that so many teachers face.

In today's 21st century classroom, we have the privilege to have a variety of learning abilities, background knowledge, and interests to participate in classroom discussions and activities. Our classrooms today are extremely diverse, and it would almost seem absurd to not meet every child's individual needs. Yet, there are so many teachers who oppose and shy away from differentiation. I have to admit that taking so many factors of differentiation into account is not an easy task. It is time-consuming, filled with formal and informal data, and constant self-doubt that the lesson you created meets every child's individual needs. But when incorporated into the classroom via assessment and instruction, student's academic achievement, as well as social emotional learning benefits, the effort is worth the initial struggle.

❖

Lesson 5: There Will Always Be Challenges and a Way to Overcome Them

Daniel Meyer, a sixth-grade self-contained teacher, has been teaching for 4 years. Daniel (like Stephanie) is a former student turned teacher. Daniel and I have kept in touch and have spoken several times over the past few years about differentiation specifically. Daniel works in a high-needs school district and has come to realize that while differentiation is certainly challenging at times, overcoming these challenges is quite rewarding—for him and his students.

Teacher Voice

Daniel Meyer, Sixth-Grade Teacher

Chandler Unified School District

Chandler, AZ

Differentiated instruction is a topic that educators have been hearing about, learning in professional development courses, and of course trying to master in their classrooms for a long time. People tend to think differentiation is difficult, when really it just requires dedicating time, thought, and practice.

I have been a teacher at a Title I school in the downtown area of a large suburb of Phoenix, AZ, for the past 4 years. Before that, I student taught at two schools in the same district but in different parts of the same suburb where it is higher on the socioeconomic ladder. At my school, we have many English Language Learners (ELLs), along with students who come from broken homes or low poverty, which calls for my colleagues and me to greatly utilize differentiated instruction in our everyday practice. Differentiation has been stressed to me since I began my teaching program, and it's still stressed today through professional development workshops and staff meetings. At first, I thought I had to alter every single student's homework or test. When, really, what I have found is when I connect with students individually, I can better assess what they need, and often students need the same thing.

For example, in one of my reading classes this year, I had a student who had moved here from El Salvador halfway through the year and didn't know any English. In getting to know her, I immediately discovered how hardworking she was and that she was determined to learn English. We worked together to decide what would be the best way for her to join our class. Ultimately, we decided that altering the content to make it accessible for her was our best option. Therefore, when our class read a story in a whole group lesson, she would listen to the story on the computer, while the rest of the class read it aloud. She was able to stop at parts when necessary to go back over something or to note when the vocabulary words of the lesson were introduced in the story and still join the rest of the class for additional activities. The interesting thing was, I found that this strategy worked well for other students, too.

(Continued)

(Continued)

Noticing these patterns has been instrumental in helping me distinguish between differentiation being difficult versus requiring time and thoughtfulness. With the population at my school and taking into consideration some of the home lives that my students have, differentiation is vital in my class. I first look at the various levels of my students through their benchmark assessments, state assessments, and other pieces of data that help me group the students for small group rotations/teaching. This past year, I had five different levels of readers to use when meeting with my five leveled groups, one of the groups being an ELL group. Within these small groups, I then differentiate the activities to meet even more needs of the students as they self-identify them. For example, some readers within a group may need more practice with their reading fluency where others need more practice with comprehension of a text. The same thing goes for math, where some students may need more practice with operations, while others are ready to apply the content to real life applications.

As Daniel points out, differentiation requires time and thought. In this process, teachers sometimes feel "stuck" because their thoughts lead them to perceived barriers like those indicated in the chart below. I offer additional considerations when one of these obstacles rears its ugly head and all of these concerns and considerations as outlined in Figure 2.4.

Throughout reading this book, you may feel new concerns or hesitations. I encourage you to reread this chapter and recall the pieces of advice I offer in the introduction and persevere.

Chapter 3 will examine the four areas where teachers can differentiate for student need and want: content, process, **product**, and learning environment. Part II will then detail the process for planning and implementing student-driven differentiation.

Figure 2.4   Differentiation Concerns and Considerations

Differentiation Concern	Considerations
I don't have time to plan something different for each student.	You do not need to plan for each individual student. Plan learning opportunities that correspond with the learning progressions of the standard(s) you are assessing. Then, use formative assessment results to flexibly group (and regroup) students with regard to where they are in the learning progression.

Differentiation Concern	Considerations
How do I manage a classroom of students all at different places?	Shift the way you look at management. The teacher can effectively manage students by giving them a clear road map for learning; then the students can be partners in managing their progress. The teacher then mixes whole group, small group, and 1:1 instruction to address the needs of students. When the learning intentions and success criteria are clear, students can take ownership of their learning and will be productive even during the times the teacher is working with other students.
What do I do with the students who "finish"?	Stop asking this question. We are never finished learning. Instead, ask yourself, what comes next? Plan for this at the beginning of the unit to be prepared for students who will need more.
What do I do with the students who aren't progressing?	The good news is, you are using evidence to alert you to the fact that students aren't learning and you have the opportunity to try something else. Focus on what you can do (*offer students different text and eliminate superfluous requirements*) rather than focus on what the student is not doing (*paying attention*).
The end of the quarter is Friday; everyone has to be done by then.	Nope. Learning does not know dates. Systems know dates. You can continue a unit of study even after a quarter date ends; it's ok. The key is how you report learning, and ensure all stakeholders understand this piece.

Discussion Questions

▶ Why do you think there is so much confusion around terms like differentiation, data, and assessment?

▶ What distinguishes student-driven differentiation from other definitions of differentiation?

▶ What role do student–teacher relationships play in regard to the role of feedback?

▶ In what ways can teachers engage school leaders in the benefits of differentiated instruction?

online resources

Visit the companion website at http://resources.corwin
.com/studentdrivendifferentiation.

Chapter 3

Four Areas to Differentiate

Figure 3.1   Four Areas to Differentiate

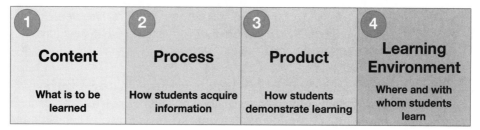

"In schools, however, we require students to learn and be good at everything, regardless of their proclivities, readiness levels, cultural barriers, learning deficiencies, or learning styles. We insist that students know how to analyze poetry, paint a picture that reflects a particular style of art, write essays, solve calculus problems, balance chemical equations, debate civic issues, remember historical events, defend their opinions about sovereign governments, use multiple computer software programs, acquire vocabulary, keep up proper hygiene, speak publicly, maintain friendships, navigate adolescence, demonstrate positive morality, ask probing questions, remember multiple tasks, organize their school supplies, and turn in their work on time- and this is just on Monday."

—Wormeli and Tomlison (2007, p. 10)

After being in any classroom for even just a few minutes, it can easily be noted that no two students present and learn in exactly the same way. With this fact in mind, Carol Ann Tomlinson coined the four categories in which teachers can examine to determine how to best differentiate instruction to meet students' needs: content (what is to be learned), process (how students acquire knowledge), product (how students demonstrate learning), and learning environment (where and with whom students learn).

> **Readiness:** student's entry point relative to particular knowledge, understanding, or skills (Tomlinson, 2014, p.18).

The teacher in a differentiated classroom thoughtfully uses assessment data to guide modifications to content, process, product, or learning environment. Content is what teachers want students to learn from a particular segment of study, or the materials or mechanisms through which the students gain access to that information. Process describes activities designed to ensure that students use key skills to make sense of, apply, and transfer essential knowledge and understandings. Products are vehicles through which students demonstrate and extend what they have learned. (Tomlinson, 2014, p.18).

More often than not, teachers must differentiate in more than one category to meet their students' needs based on their **readiness**, assessment evidence, and input directly from the student. This chapter will detail some of the most effective differentiation methods within each of the four categories and explain how student voice was considered amongst other evidence.

Content: What Is to Be Learned?

When I started teaching in 2001, curriculum was largely determined by individual teachers, and what went on in their classrooms was a mystery. I remember asking the principal who hired me (to teach middle school gifted humanities and general social studies), "What, specifically, should I teach?"

His response was, "US history." I remember thinking to myself, "Thanks for narrowing that down for me." I was shocked that there wasn't a book that told me what to teach on each and every day. I had no idea I had to decide *what* to teach. This seemed like an insurmountable task and a huge responsibility. What if I chose the wrong things? How much time should I spend on each of the topics I chose within US history? What if I taught something wrong? While I loved sociology and psychology and had taken a lot of college courses on these topics (which subsequently qualified me to teach social studies), I certainly was not a history buff.

Based on my own learning experiences, it seemed as if content drove learning. During my first few years in the classroom, I still believed this. Yet, I struggled because it was impossible for me to lecture on a topic for more than 10 minutes (I didn't have enough to say, it was boring to do, and I would go home exhausted). I also didn't know on a day-to-day basis whether or not my students were comprehending the content of my lectures. This was the crux of my decision to change my teaching practices; I wanted to gain a better understanding of where my students were without giving them study guides that looked eerily similar to tests. My practice of giving my students study guides seemed to be more of an exercise in memorization, and short-term memorization at that, than truly connecting students with the learning goal.

The practice of asking students to memorize facts is not limited to social studies. As former high school math teacher Dan Meyer says in his TED Talk, *Math Class Needs a Makeover* (2010), "To start with, I'd like to break math down into two categories. One is computation; this is the stuff you've forgotten."

To be perfectly honest, it was difficult to erect a new teaching model, and it didn't happen overnight. I didn't have an example to follow. All I knew was something needed to give. In the beginning, I was petrified when I decided not to lecture anymore. I was afraid parents would think their children weren't being exposed to copious amounts of quality content. I was worried that by giving up this instructional piece, I was undermining the role of the teacher. I was determined to figure out a way to strike a balance— have students take control of the content and ensure that they were exposed to and deeply comprehend concepts like democracy and civility, theme and plot structure, and more. Years later, I can look back and see that I didn't give up the role of the teacher, I *changed* my role to include student voice to differentiate instruction; and it was the best change I ever made as evidenced by anecdotal data (remember, you can use this type of data in conjunction with other data to make decisions) and summative data (standardized tests scores). Take for example, an anecdotal account of student-driven differentiation from Julia Mkrtychian, now a high school junior, who writes about her learning experiences in student-driven differentiation in middle school.

Standards-Aligned

As Julia articulately stated, "I believe no matter what age our generation's students are turning, it is important teachers provide resources and outlets for students to be able to acquire help and further their learning."

Fortunately (although some may disagree) for today's teachers, we have solidified sets of standards (Common Core State Standards for ELA and

Student Voice

Julia Mkrtychian, High School Junior

Skokie, IL

Based on my experiences as a student, it seems that teachers assume we, soon-to-be adults, should be learning more from the mouths of our instructors, and less from the minds of our peers. It's presentations and lectures, silent work and copying notes, and unfortunately, it repeats every day until you escape the prison we know as high school. A lot of adults may complain that we teenagers are just a bunch of babies; that our generation is just "too lazy" to work hard and that we are born with everything handed to us. Well, those statements are completely inaccurate. Although there will always be kids that want nothing to do with growing up, they aren't even close to overshadowing the excellence our generation will provide for our nation's future.

Currently, our schools care too much about satisfying the Common Core, when they should actually care about how to meaningfully further their students' knowledge even after they graduate. As a result, students focus too much on memorizing the lectures they were given, which means they most likely will forget the material in less than a few weeks. Some people complain that teenagers are just overexaggerating about how much they may hate their classes, and how difficult school is. Well, let me let you in on a little secret; it's not an overexaggeration.

First of all, let me say that in no way am I trying to sound cocky, but as a junior in high school, I haven't seen a *B* on a report card since the fourth grade. A lot of adults may say that I must be a genius, that I must be hardworking and studious. Well, I may be hardworking, but the only thing I've worked hard at is memorizing the material that has been handed to me. Unfortunately, there have been very few things I feel like I have been able to take away from my time at school, considering most of what I have learned have been from the same unenthusiastic lesson plans. In all honesty, it really is unfortunate that I'm not the only student that feels like this, especially when school and schoolwork consumes almost every hour of many people's days during the year. Of course, our lives will never be as relaxed as we want them to be, but I believe if we are forced to learn material, upon material, upon even more material, then there needs to be a method that will help students comprehend this information deeper than just its surface.

Even though it seems like I have retained a strong hatred for the educational system for several years, I can recollect fond memories of my days in middle school. I truly enjoyed middle school much more than high school. It's not because the classes were easier, the pressure to do well was far more miniscule, or because there was more time to have fun. In fact, it was because no matter which teacher you had, or which class you took, you could feel the teacher's genuine enthusiasm when they taught the class. Each teacher spent time catering to the various needs of their students, to make sure each and every one of them knew what they were supposed to know.

My seventh-grade English class was one of the best classes I had in all 11 years I have attended school. This was a class that combined individual creativity, critical thinking, and innovation into one class, just for a bunch of 13-year-olds. This is the class I continue to compare my high-school classes to, specifically because of how deeply my 13-year-old self began to understand what I was being taught, and how I would be able to use what I am learning outside of the classroom. It wasn't just "book, discussion, essay"; it was working with your peers, working with your school, and working with your community.

In particular, there was a project I distinctly remember doing that made class more than just a class. It was our group broadcasting project for the book *Fahrenheit 451* by Ray Bradbury. This book taught us so much in regard to the necessity of the First Amendment, which is more important to us now than it was 4 years ago. Our class was divided into five or six groups, each with the responsibility to create a segment for the broadcast, or design and direct the whole show. Students were given titles like "philosophers," and "lawyers," and had to conduct extremely detailed research regarding the laws and amendments that were relevant to the book, or the deeper social issues that were faced in the story. Rather than our teacher giving us some notes on the book, giving us a test, and then moving on, she understood the importance in letting students become their own detectives. She understood the importance in helping students find their own truths and allowing them to work on being their best. In the end, the students became the teachers, and they were able to not only observe the life of Guy Montag, but create their own values based on the facts and opinions they found for themselves.

At this point, I think my opinions on present-day education systems are fairly explicit. My biggest intention for writing this is because I believe no matter what age our generation's students are turning, it is important teachers provide resources and outlets for students to be able to acquire help and further their learning. Schools should not solely care about making sure their students acquire that flawless A in their class. Instead, students should be learning and remembering their class work to help them that next day, that next week, that next year. Schools shouldn't be a place where students are scared to ask for help, but instead be a place where students know they are good enough to accomplish anything. Additionally, students should never have to feel like school is the place they'll never be able to express their ideas. School should be about creating pathways for students to find what they love, and what they care about, because in the end, if schools can't do that for their students, who will?

Math, NGSS for science, NCArts, National PE Standards, C3 framework for social studies, and more). These standards are a gift as they largely focus on skills and concepts that can be mastered using a variety of content. For those standards with built-in content, there is almost always a specific skill attached to the standard (demonstrate, build, model). There are very few standards that require students to recall, memorize, or regurgitate to meet the expectation, although these actions certainly may serve a purpose in the **learning intentions** attached to the standard.

The **standards align** perfectly with student-driven differentiation. The standards allow teachers to ensure student mastery using content that is most relevant for them. But many times, giving students some control/ choice of content is difficult for teachers. The thought of giving students ownership over content can be overwhelming with the sheer abundance of content available. Plus, some teachers love the specific content they teach; it is the reason they became a teacher. And this is ok! Teachers don't need to give up the things they are passionate about, but they can use their passions to model for students what it looks like to love learning and be interested in a topic and then help students find their own passions within a content area. All students need to take US history, but not all students need to be passionate about a specific time period or event.

The good news is, there are ways you can allow student voice to drive differentiation of content while maintaining control and exposing all students to a variety of content to build a solid foundation of knowledge. It is important to remember that appropriate choice (read more about this in Chapter 8) can be offered to help give students some control of the content.

The way I recommend doing this is to create units of study based around a culminating activity (as opposed to a final product), which allows for students to have a clear vision of the learning intentions and **success criteria** and naturally lend themselves to differentiating content.

The first couple of years, it was difficult to strike a balance. I confused culminating "activity" with product. I also used too broad of categories for content. Figure 3.2 shows the evolution of using student-driven differentiation to teach the concept of the three branches of government (which fits with the learning intentions of the C3 Standard: D2.Civ.5.6-8. explain the origins, functions, and structure of government with reference to the US Constitution, state constitutions, and selected other systems of government).

When I first covered this content, my teaching focus was on students being able to recall large quantities of information on one large test. Over the years, I changed to assess student understanding of different parts of the US Constitution in smaller chunks with a culminating activity rather than a large "Constitution Test." With this change, I was able to ensure the students mastered the important content, and was able to ensure this at a much deeper level than on a 1-day test. Take, for example, the evolution of how I taught and how students learned the concept of the three branches of government in Figure 3.2.

As evident in the chart, initially, I focused way too much on what the students would do (perform on a test) rather than how they would show what they learned. In time, I realized by focusing on the content and process, differentiating for students' needs (usually in both of these categories),

Figure 3.2 Evolution of Teaching and Learning: The Three Branches of US Government

Year	Content	How did student voice determine differentiation?	Process	Culminating Activity/ Product
1	Three branches of the US Government	N/A	Textbook reading, note-taking, and worksheets	One portion of a 100-question final test
2	Checks and balances How a bill becomes a law	Students have autonomy to choose the topic of the bills they would write and the content which they would need to research to write and "sell" their bills.	Students researched their topics and wrote bills. The focus was on writing the bill, not necessarily getting it through all of the steps of how a bill becomes a law.	Students in congressional committees (small groups) each wrote a bill which one other committee would then read and determine whether or not the bill would stay alive.
3	Checks and balances How a bill becomes a law	Students have autonomy to choose the topic of the bills they would write and the content which they would need to research to write and "sell" their bills.	Most students chose topics they were interested in, and in order to write bills, they had to engage in quite a bit of research to determine how the current circumstances came to be and what hurdles they would face getting the bill to pass.	Congresswoman Jan Schakowsky from the students' district came to school and acted as the president as student congressional committees went through the entire process of drafting and passing bills into law. *Other teachers acted as a judicial branch for laws that needed to be deemed constitutional or not, which allowed for another example of checks and balances.

the end product almost guaranteed students' products exceed my expectations. Additionally, the culminating activity in Year 3 gave students an authentic audience and allowed them to role play—something that humans innately like to do. The next few chapters will detail how to incorporate various types of roleplaying, but first, to ensure a common understanding, I will define some important concepts vital to student-driven differentiation.

Learning Intentions and Success Criteria

The terms *learning intentions* and *success criteria* come from the work of John Hattie, author of *Visible Learning for Teachers: Maximizing Impact on Learning* (2012). In *Visible Learning*, Hattie shares the results of a meta-analysis of 15+ years of research involving thousands of students to provide evidence as to what really works to improve learning.

Hattie stresses that teachers and students must have a clear and shared understanding of both the learning intentions (what students are expected to learn) and success criteria (what success looks like in the end).

> The aim is to get the students actively involved in seeking this evidence: their role is not simply to do tasks as decided by teachers, but to actively manage and understand their learning gains. This includes evaluating their own progress, being more responsible for their learning, and being involved with peers in learning together about gains in learning.

Hattie then uses a driving analogy to illustrate the importance of success criteria:

> Imagine if I were simply to ask you to get in your car and drive; at some unspecified time, I will let you know when you have successfully arrived (if you arrive at all). For too many students, this is what learning feels like. (p. 56)

This last part is one that many teachers object to immediately: "Show them what success looks like? Isn't that cheating?" Or, "I don't have time to create x,y,z to show them an example success criteria." In short, no it is not. In fact, I think the opposite: If we don't show the students the success criteria or we can't easily produce an example of the success criteria, we are cheating them.

In fact, if we don't show the students the success criteria or we can't easily produce an example of the success criteria, we are cheating them.

If you are still concerned, consider the following questions, if you look at images of a garden (success criteria) on Pinterest to inform how you will plant your own garden, is that cheating? Of course not. Pinterest just gives you some ideas of what success *could* look like. Then, you take the necessary pieces (learning intentions) and arrange them in a way that demonstrates all of the success criteria.

Learning intentions should be based on the standards being assessed rather than the product that is to be "turned in." For example, solid learning intentions may ask students to construct an argument about a turning point in history identifying all of the necessary pieces of that argument (claim, evidence, support) (read more about defining learning intentions in Chapter 4). A teacher can easily show students examples of real-life artifacts that demonstrate these success criteria: blog posts, TED Talk transcripts, or articles.

Conversely, an ill-fitting learning intention requires students to create a 3D diorama of a turning point in history using required materials as now the learning intentions are focused on the production of the diorama rather than the synthesis of the information. A good rule of thumb is to ask yourself, "Can I easily produce real-life examples of a product that demonstrates all of the success criteria?" If the answer is, yes, the learning intentions and example success criteria are likely sound. If the answer is "no," perhaps, students can create dioramas? Of course. The key is for students to clearly know how they show their understanding of the learning intentions using that mechanism.

Tip: Don't be afraid of allowing students to use technology to show their learning, even if you aren't familiar with it. You are focusing on evidence of the learning intentions, not the medium.

The beauty of student-driven differentiation is that just like the Pinterest garden idea, when students have examples of success criteria, they can demonstrate the learning intentions in a variety of ways. Success criteria are used for both individual lessons and for the overall unit of study. In those schools that have adopted standards-based grading, the success criteria are the components students need to "meet" or "master" the standard.

Curriculum Compacting

Curriculum compacting, developed by Dr. Joseph Renzulli and Linda Smith in 1978, is a differentiation strategy which can benefit high-achieving students. It is a process by which evidence from pre-assessments are used to help students determine what parts of the curriculum they have already mastered. When those areas of knowledge and skills are identified, these students are exempt from relearning these concepts. Instead, they work on learning extensions (Coil, 2008).

Pre-assessments do not take into account the rate at which students acquire information. Therefore, evidence from ongoing formative assessments must be considered and appropriately acted upon to meet the needs of these students.

Figure 3.3   Examples: Student-Driven Products Demonstrating Success Criteria

	Second-Grade Science	Seventh-Grade English Language Arts
Learning intention	Demonstrate knowledge of the types of water and landforms in a particular area by developing a model to represent the shapes.	Write informative or explanatory texts to examine a topic and convey ideas, concepts, and information through the selection, organization, and analysis of relevant content.
Teacher provided worked example of success criteria demonstrating learning intentions	3D model of The Grand Canyon made with classroom supplies	Newspaper article
Student-driven product example 1 demonstrating success criteria of the learning intentions	Used SeeSaw tools to model the land and water forms in the Philippines (where his grandparents live). The student highlighted areas on a 3D model he created as he orally described them. Viewers offered this student feedback via comments (written or verbal) on SeeSaw	Letter to President Obama about extreme poverty. This student was very proud that President Obama was in office as she shared many similarities with him, and she said he gave her hope that she could be successful.
Student-driven product example 2 demonstrating success criteria of the learning intentions	Series of overlapping drawings that were cut into different shapes and put together to form a model of the Florida panhandle (where the student was going to vacation that spring). The student demonstrated this for a small group of peers to solicit feedback.	Wrote the missing chapter of *Outliers* titled "Band: Positive or Negative Impact on Academics." This student was an active participant in the symphonic band and proposed that students who played an instrument performed better academically, and wanted to prove or disprove his theory.

In my experience as both a gifted teacher and a differentiation instructional coach, curriculum compacting allows for students to grow at their own pace and work on extensions like **passion projects**, which are detailed later in this section. However, there is one caveat to curriculum compacting that teachers must be readily cognizant of as they determine how to differentiate for their students. A pre-assessment (presupposing the pre-assessment adequately assesses the skills or standards being evaluated) will only tell you a student's level of performance or knowledge base at the start of the unit. Pre-assessments do not take into account the rate at which students acquire information. Therefore, evidence from ongoing formative assessments must be considered and appropriately acted upon to meet the needs of these students. Better yet, over time, you can start to see a pattern of content acquisition with specific students, and you can identify which students are likely to master material more quickly than others.

A while back, I worked with a sixth-grade science teacher to differentiate for her high-achieving students. The teacher was regularly receiving concerned emails from parents of these students because their students were not being challenged in science. This teacher was stuck. These students were not showing mastery of concepts on pre-assessments, so she couldn't justify compacting the curriculum for them. We decided to ask the students directly, "What is going on?" The interesting thing was all four students who were asked this question replied in the same way, "We don't know the material on the pre-test. But, we can learn it in one day, on our own, just by doing the reading." According to the students, they needed the process and pacing differentiated for them.

The teacher and I decided to test out the students' input. We gave them the reading for the next unit 3 days before the pre-assessment and encouraged them to read the material before the pre-assessment, which took the form of a test. If indeed this was all the students needed in order to qualify for curriculum compacting, so be it.

And, what happened? All four of the students given the material showed mastery on the pre-assessment. More importantly the students felt their voice had been heard. Case in point, this email the teacher and I received from one of the parents who had previously emailed with great concern for his son:

The following email is based on an actual email from a parent. Names and other distinguishing factors have been changed to protect the anonymity of the parties involved.

Dear Mrs. Smith and Mrs. Westman,

Good morning! Last night at dinner, I asked my son about his day. His cheeks turned a little pink and he started to grin which usually indicates he is happy about something.

Apparently, Andrew had taken a science pretest on ecosystems and he was excited that he had performed well on this pretest! Andrew went on to explain that unlike pretests in the past, for this pretest he had been given reading material to review several days prior to the test and therefore was able to familiarize himself with the content. This way Andrew could immediately show how quickly he could pick up the content and Andrew explained that now that he had shown mastery of the material on the pretest he was given an enrichment opportunity that would allow him to go deeper in his learning.

Andrew was ecstatic and therefore my wife and I were, too. We thought we would offer you some insight into what things look like from our end and express our gratitude for giving Andrew and other students an opportunity to learn at their level right from the get-go.

Warmly,

James

This experience propelled the teacher to offer readings in advance of pre-assessments to all of her students. Then, she would compact the curriculum as indicated and offer students extensions based on their interests in the field of science. Better yet, over time and watching how students performed amend the questions on the test to assess students understanding at more complex depths of knowledge.

Varied Resources and Texts

There is quite a bit of debate over the right way to vary resources and texts for students. As stated previously, I believe teachers differentiate best when they have autonomy to determine the best way for them to reach the needs of all students. When determining appropriate text for students, many teachers choose to offer texts at varying levels and have students practice the same skills. But, this doesn't sit right with me. This reminds me of the days of leveled reading groups, and it boils down to glorified tracking within the classroom setting. Another option is to have students read same text and differentiate the skills assessed and/or tier the questions asked.

Something that always irked me (and seemingly many literature teachers) about differentiating content in literature was losing the classroom community aspect of conducting a whole class read. All students deserve access to rich, age-appropriate text and discussion of the reading even if the text may be "too difficult" for some students; that's where the student-driven differentiation piece comes into play, determining *why* the text is too difficult (lack of background knowledge, length of reading, vocabulary) and then offer appropriate scaffolds.

In Julia's vignette presented earlier in this chapter, she referenced a collaborative learning opportunity that centered on a singular reading *Fahrenheit 451*.

Using *Fahrenheit 451*, the goal was to engage the entire class in a read of a classic piece of literature, using the novel as a springboard to further differentiate subsequent, related readings, and incorporate student interest. Using information gathered during classroom discussions of *Fahrenheit 451* and student interviews, the students and I decided we would host a mock talk show with the topic being, "What would Bradbury do?" The students and I assessed which skills they had yet to master and then designed a project that allowed students to work collaboratively on tasks related to their goals. See examples of the roles, skills, and questions students focused on below. Students were each given a set of pertaining text and media. You can see how the groups were divided in Figure 3.4.

Figure 3.4   *Fahrenheit 451* Example

Group 1	Group 2
• Topic: Perception versus Reality	• Topic: Is the banning of books a violation of the First Amendment?
• Skills assessed: Reading for information, identify elements of fiction and non-fiction	• Skills assessed: Acquire and use academic vocabulary, reading for information
• Role in talk show: Production/video Crew and Hosts	• Role in talk show: Panel Attorneys
• Essential questions:	• Essential questions:
○ What is truth, and what is reality?	○ What is censorship?
○ Is perception reality?	○ Does censorship (specifically the banning of books) violate the First Amendment?
○ How does Bradbury use the idea of perception versus reality in *Fahrenheit 451?*	○ What are the legal implications of censorship and book banning?
	○ What are the social implications of censorship and book banning?
Group 3	**Group 4**
• Topic: utopia versus dystopia: Is it possible for a utopia to exist or are all utopias destined to become dystopias?	• Topic: Bradbury's business
• Skills assessed: Compare functional and informational text, determine theme in fiction and central idea in nonfiction, acquire and use academic vocabulary	• Skills assessed: Determining author's purpose, identifying theme in fiction, comparing literary works*

(Continued)

Figure 3.4   (Continued)

Group 3	Group 4
• Role in talk show: Panel Philosophers	• Role in talk show: Panel Authors
• Essential questions:	• Essential questions:
○ Can a utopia exist or by removing potential sources of "pain," or are utopias destined to become dystopias?	○ What was Bradbury's reason for writing this book?
○ Is there a real-life dystopia?	○ What is the theme of *Fahrenheit 451*?
○ Does one need contrast to be able to appreciate?	○ What is the theme of *The Veldt*?
	○ How does the theme of *Fahrenheit 451* compare (or contrast) to the theme of *The Veldt*?

Group 5	Group 6
• Topic: How does what is going on around us affect our writing?	• Topic: Was Bradbury a visionary?
• Skills assessed: Determining historical context in fiction and nonfiction and reading for information	• Skills assessed: Using context clues and foreshadowing to make predictions, reading for information, comparing literary works
• Role in talk show: Panel Historians	• Role in talk show: Panel Detectives
• Essential questions:	• Essential questions:
○ Identify the time period that *Fahrenheit 451* was written. What was going on in the United States and the world during this time and just prior to the writing of this book?	○ What ideas was Bradbury correct in predicting?
○ What specific historical references are apparent in the book?	○ What areas was Bradbury incorrect in predicting?
	○ How did Bradbury know what the future would be like?

Process: How Students Acquire Knowledge

"Children must be taught how to think, not what to think."

—Margaret Mead

Process refers to how students acquire information. In my experience, there is a very simple way to determine how to differentiate the process for students: Ask them how.

Student voice in conjunction with formative assessment evidence will detail how teachers can differentiate the pace of instruction, challenge students by asking questions at varying depths, offer feedback at different levels, and group students.

Pacing

When used correctly, assessment for learning, or formative assessment, lets teachers know exactly where students are in their learning progression. To actually be considered formative assessment, the evidence gathered from the assessments must be used to inform instruction. And, inevitably what teachers learn is that *pacing* (how quickly students are moved through the learning intentions and demonstrate the success criteria) can vary largely. My solution to this dilemma goes back to the original premise for student-driven differentiation—plan learning experiences that account for pacing differences and embed learning paths for groups of students. Then, within these structures, allow student voice to drive the learning (see mock trial example in Chapter 6).

Effective Questioning

Similar to considering students' academic and affective needs when providing structures for cooperative learning, taking into account student needs when being asked questions also demonstrates respect for them as learners and differentiates the process for them.

Gifted and Talented teacher and coordinator Jennifer Marten, PhD, from Plymouth, Wisconsin, often cautions educators to consider the difference between *asking questions* and *questioning.* Jen recently wrote to me in an email,

> As teachers, we ask questions all day long, but how often do we stop to think about what we're asking? Are questions planned and mindful or are they surface and random? Questioning should be an important part of lesson planning as it allows us to focus on deep rather than surface learning. (Marten, 2017)

Using some of the strategies in the section below (like inner-outer circle) allows teachers to ask students effective questions, while simultaneously differentiating for their need.

In *High Impact Instruction* (2013), author Jim Knight identifies the different type, kind, and level as illustrated with examples in Figure 3.5.

Type: Right/Wrong or Opinion

Kind: Open or Closed

Level: Know, Understand, Do (Knight, 2013, pp. 153–163).

Figure 3.5   Types, Kinds, and Levels of Questions

Question Example	Type Right/wrong or Opinion	Kind Open or Closed	Level Know, Understand, Do
What is 2+2?	r/w	closed	know
Which is heavier: a pound of feathers or a pound of bricks?	r/w	open	understand
What is the most significant political event in the 20th century?	opinion	closed	understand
How did the outcome of WWI influence the start of WWII?	r/w	open	understand
You have a plate, an egg, and a bottle of water. You want to separate the egg yolk from the egg white and only have these tools. What do you do?	opinion	open	do

I often work with teachers in coaching cycles to improve the quality of questioning. During a lesson observation, we take data on the type, kind, and level of questions asked. In doing so, I have found the most powerful piece of data collected involves the student response to questions which can be seen by looking at two things: (1) the number of students who have an opportunity to respond and (2) the number of students who volunteer to respond.

Lecture-style classes give the fewest amount of opportunities for students to respond and also generally solicits the least amount of student volunteers to answer. The most efficient and effective type of questioning occurs during structured cooperative learning activities when students have an opportunity to answer open-ended, right/wrong questions at the understand or do level. The next section will identify structures that lend themselves to engaging all students in learning, while also addressing other instructional criteria.

The Whole Child

"It is YOUR professional judgment, your ingenuity, your creativity, and your passion that most impacts the whole child mosaic."

—Dr. Dane Delli

If you have ever gotten stuck in a traffic jam or spilled coffee on yourself on the way to work, you are familiar with walking into your classroom pre-occupied. Similarly, if you have ever been asked to fill out a form (perhaps a curriculum map) that was organized in a way that was foreign to you, you know all too well the feeling of frustration of being forced to do something that hurts your brain.

Our students are no different. In fact, some of our students come to school chronically preoccupied and leave with their heads spinning. This is because we often don't address our students' affective and **metacognitive needs** in addition to their academic needs, because we forget that we have permission to do so.

In August of 2017, I had the pleasure of hearing Dr. Dane Delli, Superintendent of Glenview School District 34, in Glenview, Illinois, welcome his teachers back to school. Dane's welcome resonated loudly with the audience, in large part because of one statement in particular. Dane said,

> I believe that, while we must understand that we live in a standards-based environment and while tests scores matter, it is YOUR professional judgment, your ingenuity, your creativity, and your passion that most impacts the whole child mosaic.

Being attentive to the whole child is the foundation on which student-driven differentiation is built. Some of the ways we can attend to the whole child are to incorporate movement into learning, use, and explicitly explain metacognitive strategies, and use evidence of students' affective (social-emotional) needs to inform instruction.

Incorporating movement into instruction has proven to be an effective strategy for energizing the brain and creating desired learning conditions. As Eric Jensen writes in *Teaching With the Brain in Mind* (2005) there are, "strong connections between physical education, movement, breaks, recess, energizing activities, and improved cognition. It demonstrates that movement can be an effective cognitive strategy to (1) strengthen learning, (2) improve memory and retrieval, and (3) enhance learner motivation and morale" (p. 60).

Figure 3.6   Nine Ways to Get Students Up and Moving

9 WAYS
TO GET STUDENTS UP AND MOVING

Musical Think, Pair, Share

Students silently walk around the room while a song related to the content/topic is playing. When the music stops, students high-five a partner, and the teacher asks a question. Students discuss the answer to the question with their partner. Some groups can share with the whole class. Repeat.

Silent Walk

Students use whiteboards, paper, or iPads to record answers. They silently walk the perimeter of the classroom and share their answers with others. Student can only use non-verbals (facial expressions and hand signals) to acknowledge their classmates' answers and show agreement, disagreement, or uncertainty.

Inner Outer Circle

Students form two circles. The inner circle faces out and the outer circle faces in so that students are looking at each other. Students answer questions posed by the teacher or a student facilitator. For each question, students on the outside rotate clockwise. The inner circle does not rotate. Activity works well in a hallway or building foyer.

Four Corners

Each corner of the room represents a different thought, idea, or answer. Students move to the corner that best represents them. Each corner group discusses the topic, and then a representative from each group shares with the larger group.

Opinion Line-Up

Students form a human Likert scale to show how strongly they agree or disagree with a statement.

Gallery Walk

Students respond to prompts, visuals, or other artifacts posted around the room with written comments (butcher paper works well as a background). Students rotate through the gallery twice so that they can respond and see their classmates' responses.

Snowball Toss

Students write their answer to a question on a piece of paper. Then, they crumple up the paper and gently toss the "snowball" across room. Students pick up a tossed "snowball" and share the answer they picked.

Partner Match

Create four categories related to the content being covered. (i.e., square, triangle, circle, rectangle). Have students find a classmate to be their partner for each of the categories. Throughout the unit, have students meet up with their various partners for additional activities.

Visualize Your Learning

Using whiteboards, paper, or 1:1 device students create a visual (drawing, symbol, quote, or phrase) to describe their thoughts on the topic at hand. Students then walk around the room and share with each other.

As teachers we frequently say things to students which mean absolutely nothing to them. One of the best examples of this is when teachers tell students to "study." While well-intentioned, students are not born knowing what it means to study. Instead of asking students to study, we must focus on how they learn and help them recognize their metacognitive needs.

Unfortunately for me, I didn't understand how I learn best until I became an adult learner and was given the autonomy to "study" as I saw fit. As it turns out, making flashcards and writing outlines were not the most effective strategies for me. But, creating mind maps and visual depictions are highly effective for me.

With the availability of research about learning, our students have the opportunity to ascertain how they learn best now, as children. The key is for educators to recognize and embrace the fact that all students do not react the same way to all learning strategies. Therefore, we should avoid requiring students to use a certain strategy (take notes), and instead expose them to a variety of learning strategies and help them determine what strategies were helpful or not. Then, we can tap into this knowledge to choose/differentiate learning strategies for subsequent learning activities.

Assessing and documenting students' affective needs and growth (commonly referred to as social emotional) is as important as assessing and documenting students' academic progress according to the National Education Technology Plan Update released by the US Department of Education in January 2017 (www.tech.ed.org).

The plan reports some small advances in data collection and curricula addressing social-emotional learning, but stresses there is still a profound need for more reliable and relevant tools (both the learning and data collection pieces). Video learning is one way to address this deficit. As an instructional coach, I have learned that all teachers, including me, have blind spots in their practice. Chances are students do not have an accurate picture of their performance either. Video can help illustrate this. Keeping in mind our students organically record much of what they do, and video is a proven effective learning **tool** (for adults), educators can capitalize on this set of circumstances to better meet our students' social-emotional learning needs.

Video Logistics:

1. Use any device with video recording capabilities. You can use multiple devices simultaneously.

2. Set the devices up in the location(s) you wish to record (whole class, small group, individual student desks).

3. Store videos in an accessible, but not public, location (Google Drive, Flash Drive, YouTube listed as a private).

Learning Logistics:

1. Student(s) record themselves for a predetermined portion of a lesson that is likely to garner the best evidence. (See Figure 3.7 for suggestions.)

2. Teacher and student(s) confer to identify the skill they want focus on (i.e., appropriate communication with peers).

3. Teacher and student(s) co-create a list of look-fors for the skill to be observed (i.e., ineffective versus effective communication of ideas) and cite examples of each criterion: "you are wrong" versus "I see things a different way. Let me explain."

4. Teacher and student(s) co-create a data collection tool or rubric that specifies look-fors. The simpler, the better; tally systems work very nicely.

5. Student(s) and teacher watch the videos and collect data (separately).

6. Teacher and student review their findings and set a reasonable, quantifiable goal (i.e., ratio of effective to ineffective comments is 3:1).

7. Any differences in understanding could be discussed further by reviewing parts of the video together and comparing examples to the rubric.

8. The teacher and student(s) determine an action plan that includes a learning piece.

9. After a predetermined interval of learning, the teacher and student(s) repeat the process and determine next steps (adjust action plan to continue to work toward goal or determine the goal is met and set a new goal).

An additional bonus of having students use video to self-assess their affective qualities is they have additional opportunities to interact with the content of lesson when they watch their recordings.

This model does not have to be used with all students at the same time, nor do all students need to have the same look-fors/data collection tools. This method can be differentiated to meet the social-emotional learning needs of individual students just as we differentiate for students' academic needs.

Figure 3.7   Seven Ways to Use Video Recording in the Classroom

HIGH-IMPACT
7 WAYS
TO USE VIDEO
RECORDING IN
THE CLASSROOM

Self-Assess Social Emotional Competencies

Video can be used to help students understand their social-emotional strengths and areas for growth. Teachers and students can collaboratively create a student skills rubric to collect data, set goals, and track progress.
BONUS: This approach also gives students an additional opportunity to engage with the content of the lesson.

Solicit Feedback

With the increase of social media and YouTube use, students are frequently asking for and giving others feedback. Tap into this natural inclination by providing learning about how to give and ask for feedback appropriately and how to determine whether or not feedback should be considered.

As Formative Assessment

Short video clips can be used to evaluate how students are performing in relation to the learning intention(s). Students can record short oral responses, demonstrations, and examples to be shared with their teachers and/or peers.

To Track Progress

Students can document their progress toward a goal by creating a series of video clips that illustrate their growth.

················· To Demonstrate Learning ·················

 Students can use video as a medium for their success criteria*. They can create short movies, PSA's, stop-motion films, cartoons, music videos, and a variety of other options to show their learning in a relevant method of their choosing.

························· To Compare ·························

Teachers can use student video in PLCs/team meetings to compare student work and instructional practices.

····················· Find a Need and Fill It ·····················

 Teachers often do not have an accurate perception of their teaching practices. Video recordings can help teachers gain a more clear and comprehensive view of their work, which can be used to set and achieve professional goals.

*Terminology from *Visible Learning for Teachers* by John Hattie

---

Product: How Students Demonstrate Learning

As mentioned earlier, frequently well intended, teachers place too much emphasis on the final product. There are many reasons why this is the case, one being that we often feel the need to have something to *show* our students have learned. We want to cover bulletin boards, we want pretty classrooms for open house, and therefore we require end products to *look pretty*. When, really, learning is not always pretty. Sometimes, it is very messy. While there are times when tangible final products are necessary, and therefore, quality craftsmanship should be a consideration, this is not always the case. Sometimes a final product isn't necessary at all because formative assessment can show mastery of a skill or concept without being an elaborate undertaking.

For example, let's go back to my 1st year teaching in 2001. I remember assigning students the following: "Create a poster depicting a battle from World War II. Posters must be on a poster or tri-fold board."

Looking back, I am happy to see that I offered my students some "choice" although I now realize this choice was anything but a choice that included student voice (more on this in Chapter 8). I was focused on having something that the students created. A project. I didn't wind up getting a whole lot of outstanding projects as (1) many of my students focused on the end result and not the learning process, and (2) many of my students felt stuck and disengaged as they were asked to demonstrate their learning in a way that was not suitable for them. I never assigned that project again. In fact, I realized that students didn't need to focus on the battles of World War II unless they wanted to; perhaps, there was another facet of World War II that piqued their interest and that was their focus (economics, sociology, technology) and focused on critical-thinking skills using World War II as content.

When determining whether or not to differentiate the product for students, consider doing the following:

▶ Conference with students to find out how they would ideally like to show their learning (written, using technology, creating something tangible). Then, work with them to determine *specific criteria* aligned with the *learning intentions* for their product.

▶ Offer differentiated product options (see Figure 3.8). You can differentiate product type (poster, podcast, TED Talk) and product requirements (length, group make-up, medium).

▶ Suggest material and mediums instead of requiring them.

Figure 3.8   Differentiated Product Options

Presentation: In front of class, video reflection, interview/conversation with an expert	*Artistic:* collage, drawing, graphic novel, sketchnote, infographic, book jacket, calendar
Written: paper, blogpost, letter to someone, email to someone, story	

Learning Environment: Where and With Whom Students Learn

If teaching is an art form, then the learning environment is the canvas. The learning environment encompasses where and with whom students learn. It includes tangible things like furniture, technology, and how students are placed in classes and less tangible things like what we value about learners and the process of learning.

Erecting an appropriate learning environment (both tangible and intangible elements) is vital to the success of student-driven differentiation. While we can differentiate the learning environment for an individual's or group of students' needs, what we need to do is ensure our learning environment is differentiated from the learning environment in which we were schooled right from the get-go. Therefore, Chapter 7 is dedicated to creating thriving learning environments.

But . . . We Have to Use a Textbook!

While all of the above information may seem like a good idea on paper, there is one perceived barrier that tends to get in the way of letting student voice drive differentiation: the textbook. Teachers (myself included) often feel that when a textbook is mandated, teacher autonomy is thrown out the window. In the Shark Tank example in Chapter 6, I share an example of how my colleague and I meshed the two together. Below, read how one school administrator, Mike Andriulli, has addressed this concern with his teachers.

Administrator's Voice

Mike Andriulli, Principal

Wayne Township Public Schools

Wayne, NJ

Nothing destroys the momentum of curriculum development like the question, "Have we decided which textbook series we are using?" All of the momentum, and most of the professional growth gained through the process, is sucked out of the room at that moment. My curriculum colleagues and I ensure that all curriculum revision is accompanied by extensive and focused professional development centered around differentiation, student

(Continued)

(Continued)

choice, strategic technology integration, and subject-specific pedagogical strategies. The curriculum is designed to be flexible and adaptable in order to allow the needs of individual learners in each classroom to drive the learning experiences. But far too often this dynamic resource gets stored on a shelf, or saved in the cloud, and is replaced by a mandated textbook series.

Any textbook series, even the most pedagogically sound, has one inherent flaw—it does not know *your* students. It may offer options for diverse learners, practice worksheets and games, a variety of leveled assessments, etc. But unlike a quality teacher, it has not fostered valuable insight into the social, emotional, and academic needs of each and every student in his or her care. Teachers have to trust these relationships, along with their training and expertise, when writing curriculum and planning student-centered learning activities.

Despite the abundance of online tools and resources available to educators to meet needs of their students, many don't feel completely secure unless they have a textbook series to follow. I have always viewed the reliance on textbooks as the life vest of education. The problem with a life vest is that you cannot learn to swim effectively with one on. You may feel secure, you may feel a boost in confidence, knowing that there is something standing between you and drowning. But the downside is, a life vest holds you back from actually trusting yourself in learning to swim. The first few times you swim without one will make you uneasy and nervous, but there is nothing more empowering than shedding that life vest and learning, instead, to be confident in your own ability to swim.

This phenomenon became abundantly clear while I was meeting with a second-year teacher during her pre-observation conference. After talking for several minutes, I asked her to reflect on the progress of her students through the first part of the year. I was impressed with how well she was able to concisely describe the students in her class, their current levels of understanding, and their individual strengths and areas for growth. As we began to plan for the lesson, I asked a simple, yet deceptively complicated, question, "What do you want your students to be able to do as a result of this lesson?" She explained the general mathematics skill and objective, but I was not totally satisfied with her answer. I pressed for more. I brought in some of the insight she provided me about her students, and, in order to facilitate a learning experience tailored to them, asked a series of questions:

- "What activities will you present to students that will allow them to work toward your intended learning outcome?"
- "What information and prompting will have to come from you?"

- "What specific supports will some students require?"
- "How will students show you they got it?"

These questions, and her thoughtful responses, resulted in a solid student-centered lesson plan. However, I could still sense a bit of doubt on her face. A few seconds later, I heard the dreaded, "But that's not how the book explains it—is that okay?" She was taken aback by my response, "Who cares?" The relief was immediate. The life vest was off, and she felt free to swim and explore the vast waters.

When used as a supplemental resource, a textbook series can clarify learning targets and provide structure for both students and teachers. It can serve as a source of comprehension questions, problem-solving tasks, and extension activities. However, teachers sometimes need "permission" to move away from the textbook series as the lone curriculum, pacing guide, and all-encompassing resource. As educators transition toward a more student-driven approach, it is imperative for district and school leaders to support and empower teachers through the process.

By utilizing strategic planning techniques, teachers can ensure their lessons remain focused on clear learning goals and, more importantly, on the individual needs of their students. It is important to develop learning experiences that offer students multiple entry points to make the content accessible and relevant. These experiences should be open-ended and provide opportunities for students to develop concepts, make connections, and consider new questions. Differentiated learning pathways should allow students to approach and apply concepts in new and innovative ways, while receiving the support they require.

Discussion Questions

▶ What are some ways you can use student voice, choice, and interest to drive differentiation of content for your students?

▶ How can curriculum compacting allow for student-driven differentiation?

▶ Beside students' academic need, what other considerations should teachers make to differentiate the process of learning?

▶ How can student voice drive this decision-making process?

▶ What role do textbooks play in teaching and learning?

Visit the companion website at http://resources.corwin
.com/studentdrivendifferentiation.

Part II

Implementation

Chapter 4

Planning Student-Driven Differentiation

"Children are very resilient learners, but ultimately, they learn and flourish best when they learn in their own style and at their own pace. The educator's highest calling is to help each child discover what those are."

—Anonymous, profoundly gifted student

As with most things, planning student-driven differentiation becomes easier and more efficient the more times you do it. I have broken down the planning into an eight-part road map that helps isolate the different components of meeting students' academic, social-emotional, and metacognitive needs using a variety of types of evidence including, most importantly, formative assessment data and student voice.

The steps that follow are intended to help you and your grade-level or department colleagues efficiently collaborate to plan and implement successful student-driven differentiated learning experiences, but they are flexible to fit your own planning style and personality. Additionally, a graphic organizer of sorts is provided at the end of the chapter to help guide your planning, should this strategy work for you or members of your team.

Figure 4.1   Student-Driven Differentiation Road Map

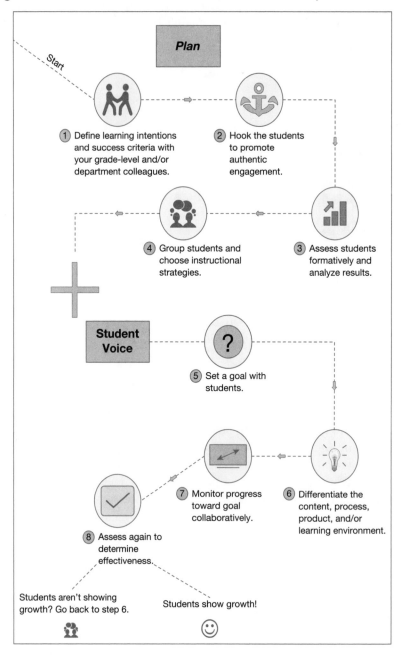

Step 1: Define

The first step in student-driven differentiation is to clearly and collaboratively define learning intentions and success criteria with your grade-level and/or content area colleagues. This is often the hardest step . . . not the defining part, the collaboration part. Full disclosure, collaborating has not always been easy for me. I like to be in control. For a long time, I mistakenly viewed collaborating with colleagues as relinquishing control. At first, it seemed foreign to me to *share* my ideas and my work with colleagues to determine our students' needs. Over time, however, I recognized that collaborating with my colleagues helped ensure high quality instruction and better-engaged students and elicited academic and affective student growth. I also realized that I felt like a better teacher. My efficacy had increased, because I no longer made decisions in isolation. I had other knowledgeable, skilled practitioners to bounce ideas off of on a daily basis. We could hypothesize, together, what our obstacles are, and together, determine an appropriate course of action. Work done in teams ranks as the #1 highest effect size according to Hattie's meta-analysis. In other words, not only is teamwork good for teachers to achieve goals, but it is *good for our students*.

Step 2: Hook

Begin each unit of study with an authentic (relevant to students) **hook** that immediately grabs students' attention and illustrates the learning intentions. One of my favorite examples of this was a teacher who created a student-driven differentiated learning opportunity for her seventh-grade students whose learning intention was to determine gratuities. The teacher, Diane Miller from McCracken Middle School in Skokie, Illinois, showed her students a short clip of an episode from a very popular sitcom during which six friends were trying determine a tip based on their bill . . . and struggled to do so. The clip was funny, totally appropriate, and very believable. Now that the students were hooked, Diane asked her essential question: How can percent help you understand situations involving money?

To plan a successful hook, ask yourself:

▶ Why do students need to learn this?

▶ How can I make this (content, skill, concept) relevant to their lives?

Then, answer these questions in the simplest of forms. If answers are not readily apparent to you (the teacher), they will be even more elusive to the students.

Finally, provide an effective thinking prompt (see Figure 4.2) to encourage students to engage with the content, ask questions, discuss with each other, rather than tell them what they will learn.

Figure 4.2 Thinking Prompt Options

Clip(s) of a tv show or movie	An image	A quote
A meme	A social media feed	A song
An infographic	A portion of an interview	A passage from a book
A mystery box filled with a variety of thinking prompts	A short (opinionated) editorial or blogpost	A message from someone outside the class (using video or Skype)

The Connection Between the Hook and Direct Instruction

Hooking students typically occurs during direct instruction time. Direct instruction often gets a bad rap because it is wrongly associated with lecturing. Lecturing is a form of **direct instruction** (the explicit teaching of a skill set or concept), but not the most effective form (there is little check for understanding, no differentiation, and can often be disengaging). But, there is a time and place for direct instruction, and a way to do it correctly. Teacher Cathy Boland often engages in direct instruction and then gives students an opportunity to engage in group or individual work.

While teaching a unit on waves and electromagnetic radiation, Cathy and her department colleague, Sean Gormley, focused on the Next Generation Science Standard MS-PS4-2: Develop and use a model to describe that waves are reflected, absorbed, or transmitted through various materials.

Cathy decided to hook the students with a variety of multimedia sources on both electromagnetic waves and the power of feedback. By using a variety of hooks, Cathy quickly built excitement around the learning intentions and clarified the success criteria. By the end of her introduction, the students were eager to build the wave model and find out if the feedback they gave their peers would have the same result on their learning as Austin had experienced in the video.

Step 3: Assess and Analyze

One of my favorite stories is about the man who taught his dog to whistle. The man was so proud of his teaching. He walked his dog around town and proudly proclaimed, "I taught my dog to whistle!"

Then, one day, a neighbor stops the man and says, "I don't hear your dog whistling."

To which the man responds, "I said I taught him to whistle, I didn't say he learned how to whistle."

Formative Assessment Ensures Students Are Learning

For many years, assessment was used as a measure to inform teachers and students how students performed in comparison to each other at arbitrary points in time. Thankfully, with years of research and a shift in the way teaching and learning is approached, the recommended method of determining student success is by using assessment to measure growth. The focus has shifted to student learning rather than teachers teaching. Assessment results are no longer final verdicts for students, but rather information for them and their teachers on where to go next. This is known as *assessment for learning*. Assessment for learning is the process of seeking and interpreting evidence for use by learners and their teachers to decide where the learners are in their learning, where they need to go, and how best to get there.

The key is to use the evidence gathered to inform instruction rather than just collecting data for the sake of collecting data. Rick Stiggins and his co-authors explain formative assessment as something that,

> happens while learning is still underway. These are the assessments that we conduct throughout teaching and learning to diagnose student needs, plan for next steps in instruction, provide students with feedback they can use to improve the quality of their work, and help students see and feel in control of their journey to success. (As quoted in Ainsworth & Viegut, 2015, p. 31)

Pre-assessments give teachers a starting point, and ongoing formative assessment helps teachers set the pace and choose content and strategies for students as they progress in their learning. Too often, educators believe they are using formative assessment correctly when in all actuality they are not. The most common misuses of formative assessment include:

▶ Collecting data (evidence) from formative assessment, but not using the data to inform instruction

▶ Not adapting pacing or differentiating for students who need modifications or extensions

▶ Assessing criteria not associated with the learning intention (i.e., assessing content recall when the learning target is a skill)

▶ Focusing on arbitrary dates to finish learning, like "end of quarter"

There are many resources available that give options for formative assessment types and creative ways to give quizzes, written responses, thumbs up/thumbs down, and so on to formatively assess students (see Figure 4.3). The key is not to just give formative assessments, but to use the information they provide and share that information with students by giving them timely and appropriate feedback. Therefore, when determining what type of formative assessment to use, ask yourself these questions:

Figure 4.3   Items That Can Be Used to Garner Formative Assessment Evidence

Conversation	Infographics
Written work	Screencasts
Tests	Video recordings of group work
Quizzes	
Video reflections	Whiteboards
Drawings	Web-based games
Performance	Instructional strategies like those in Figure 3.6
Demonstration	

▶ What am I trying to assess (skill, standard, understanding of concept)?

▶ What type of assessment is most likely to assess this (multiple choice, performance assessment, written response)?

▶ Where does the student need to go next?

▶ How will I use the information from the formative assessment to adapt my next steps?

> The key is not to just give formative assessments, but to use the information they provide and share that information with students by giving them timely and appropriate feedback.

Offering the Right Feedback Is Key

The ability for teachers to provide timely, relevant, and actionable **feedback** to students is critical for their success in the classroom and also is the most prominent force in allowing student voice to drive the differentiation. In addition to a strong relationship, the feedback in and of itself must be considered (see Figure 4.4). Feedback done right is reciprocal; it should enable the student to go deeper, and simultaneously inform the teacher's next steps. Most importantly, feedback is most likely to be applied when students and teachers have genuine relationships (see Figure 1.1 Three Tenets of Forming Genuine Relationships With Students).

Figure 4.4   Characteristics of Feedback

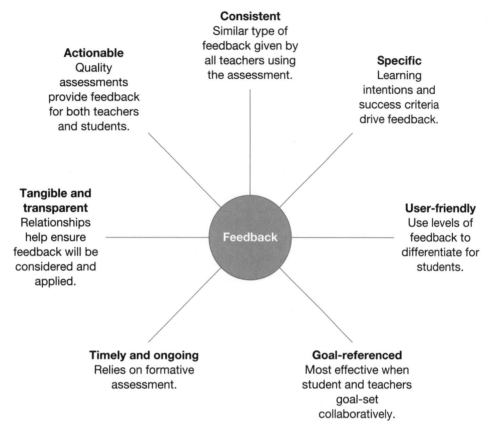

Consistent
Similar type of feedback given by all teachers using the assessment.

Actionable
Quality assessments provide feedback for both teachers and students.

Specific
Learning intentions and success criteria drive feedback.

Tangible and transparent
Relationships help ensure feedback will be considered and applied.

Feedback

User-friendly
Use levels of feedback to differentiate for students.

Timely and ongoing
Relies on formative assessment.

Goal-referenced
Most effective when student and teachers goal-set collaboratively.

The majority of teachers tend to give task-based feedback only: scores, grades, and progress toward a standard never help students get to the point of self-regulation where they can determine what they need next. This is because we often view feedback as "formal" when really it can be informal and brief in nature. Additionally, there is a false belief that all group members need to be given feedback simultaneously or individually. Rather, teachers can give students feedback in a variety of ways. Figure 4.5 offers a menu of options for giving students feedback, individually, in pairs, small groups, and so on.

In all likelihood, you will adopt many of these approaches to giving feedback and grouping as you formatively assess students and monitor their growth toward the identified learning intentions.

Effect Size

In *Visible Learning* (2012), John Hattie reports results from a synthesis of over 800 meta-analyses relating to student achievement in the form of an effect size. Criteria with a score above 0.4 are considered to have the greatest impact of student learning, with a 0.4 being roughly equivalent to 1 year's growth with 1 year of correct implementation.

Figure 4.5   Ways to Give Students Feedback

- Write them a short note.
- Annotate assignments.
- Use technology to give verbal feedback (GAFE, Otus, Voxer).
- Use technology to give verbal and visual feedback (Screencastify, SeeSaw).
- Use chat features on technology.
- Chat with students in person.
- While they are working on a task, point to something and ask them a clarifying question.
- Put a Post-it with a smiley face next to them as they work.
- Ask students for other ideas of how you can communicate feedback to them.

One of the most remarkable experiences I have had watching both student and teacher growth was in an instructional coaching cycle with teacher Jim Bruton. Jim and I partnered around his goal to use leveled feedback. In Jim's vignette, you can see how one student in particular improved as a writer by responding to recursive cycles of feedback.

Teacher Voice

Jim Bruton, Sixth-Grade English Language Arts Teacher

Skokie School District

Skokie, IL

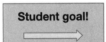

Student goal!

This past school year, my students wrote autobiographical narratives about a time that changed them. One particular student, we'll call her Afsha, wrote hers about friends she had made online who impacted her life, but stopped talking to her. Because of its content, *Afsha did not want to write her narrative in paragraph form, but rather as a series of forum posts and messaging chats interspersed with her inner monologue.* It was brilliant and far beyond what I expected from a typical sixth-grade student. Afsha had tremendous insights and weaved her narrative with her nontraditional storytelling style beautifully. Because of the format she chose, Afsha's work did not meet all the requirements of the assignment (such as formatting paragraphs and having proper sentence structure). However, she had previously demonstrated her ability to write traditional prose, so we ran with it. *The key word here being, **we**.* I knew I was going to need to do something different for Afsha, but I didn't want to make this decision for her; I wanted her input to determine the best way to extend this assignment *for her goals*.

With the help and support of my differentiation coach and our librarian, we checked out novels written in similarly untraditional fashion, such as *TTYL* and *This Journal Belongs to Ratchet*, which served as models for Afsha's writing. At first, Afsha was hesitant to work toward such a different piece of writing from what her peers were doing, but she soon began to love it, and she ended up writing more than she could have ever anticipated. With continued support and coaching, her final product was incredible.

A few months later, when my students were beginning to write their mystery narratives, I knew Afsha already possessed the ability to write well beyond that of a typical sixth-grade student. As a class, we focused a lot on characterization, and on the first day of drafting. Afsha had already demonstrated her ability to create a complex character with tremendous depth and some mature ideas. Rather than have her work towards the prescribed curriculum, she and I teamed up with our differentiation coach to develop an individualized plan for writing for Afsha. The plan included continuing to develop characters, with the assumption that eventually a story would take shape. Afsha created several different documents, each with a new character. She began color-coding her writing to help herself keep track of things. As a team, we decided that she would work toward writing a much longer narrative piece, possibly turning it into a novel. She loved the idea and continued to write. The differentiation coach and I checked in on her periodically, provided feedback, and offered guidance where needed. Although a gifted writer, as a sixth-grade student, she had some difficulty trying to fit all of her pieces together to create a cohesive story of such magnitude. Feedback became extremely important so that true instruction and differentiation could occur.

Example of student-driven differentiated process: one student was seeking feedback about foreshadowing in her writing, while the other students were strengthening the reading skill of identifying foreshadowing in a story.

As Afsha's story began to take shape, we worked on additional high-level skills, such as including foreshadowing in her writing. She tried it with moderate success. She explained her thinking, and we offered more feedback and some further instruction. She continued to work at it, and continued to improve her writing, which now included some foreshadowing.

It was now time to make our feedback loop even more authentic. Afsha put together a handful of pieces of her writing that she thought included her foreshadowing and some key components of her plot. She presented these pieces to her classmates. She explained what she was working toward, and she taught the class about foreshadowing. Her classmates read her writing and provided genuine feedback. Each student made a prediction about what he or she thought would happen in the story in order to see if Afsha's foreshadowing had been successful. The students also provided feedback regarding which character they were able to most identify with and other thoughts on the story. This activity ended up turning into a lively class discussion led by

Afsha. The other students were engaged, while providing valuable feedback for a fellow student (see Figure 4.6). Afsha collected their written feedback. With the help of the differentiation coach, she was able to make sense of the feedback and use it to further develop her writing.

This authentic feedback from classmates, in addition to the feedback from myself and the differentiation coach throughout the process, helped Afsha become a more successful writer. However, none of this feedback would have been possible if we hadn't first taken into account her needs. From the information gathered from her previous writing to listening to her needs during our discussions, we were able to include her as an integral agent in her own learning. Through this process, she not only grew as a writer, but she also gained tremendous confidence in herself. She has continued to work on her novel during the summer and into her seventh-grade year.

Step 4: Group Students Strategically

Being cognizant of how students are expected to work in groups is a hallmark of student-driven differentiation. The idea of one student doing all of the work and one student being a shrinking violet is ultimately not considering student voice. When teachers are considerate of students' academic and affective needs and ensure all students have equal and appropriate

Figure 4.6   Feedback Forms and Results

Student–Student Feedback Form
1. Does the story have a clear setting? _____ Yes _____ No
Explain:
2. Does the story have a clear conflict? _____ Yes _____ No
What is the main conflict?
3. Does your partner change in the story? _____ Yes _____ No
How did your partner change in the story?
4. Is it clear what caused him or her to change? _____ Yes _____ No
What caused him or her to change?
5. Was the story interesting and engaging? _____ Yes _____ No
What was the most interesting part? Why?
6. Was there anything you were confused about in their story? _____ Yes _____ No
Explain:

Peer Feedback Form
Created by Afsha and Mr. Bruton

You are the detective!

Make a prediction about what may happen next in the story:

What evidence leads you to believe this (cite text evidence from the story):

Do you feel a connection to any of the characters? If so, circle which one, and explain *why*.
Beatrice   **Sebastian**   **Marceline**   **Isaac**

As I continue to write this story, do you have any recommendations for me?

Analyzing Students' Feedback

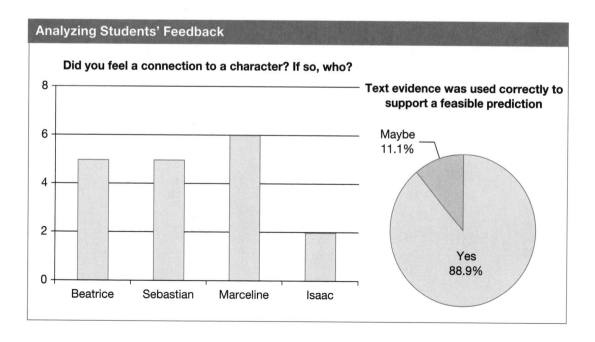

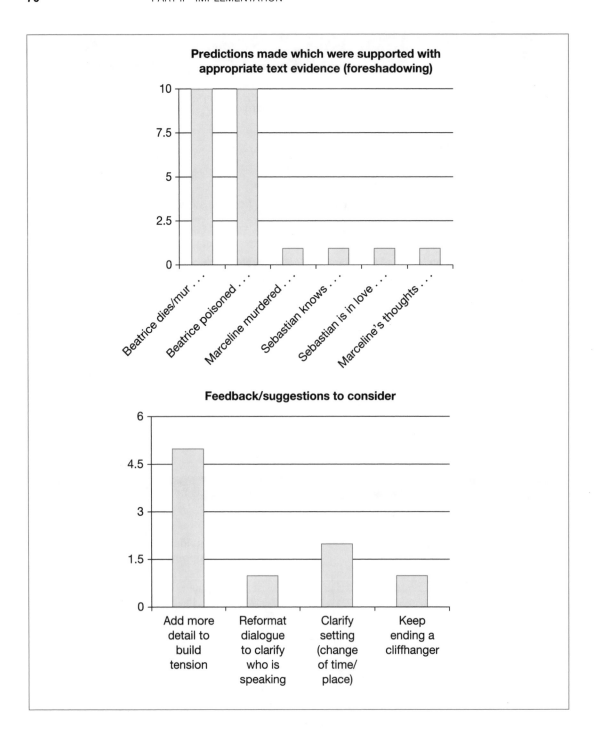

Afsha identified the following next steps
(example of student self-regulation):

☐ I will continue writing over summer and potentially into seventh grade.

☐ I will change formatting to better clarify setting change.

☐ I will elaborate on details to add more suspense.

☐ I can continue to share and ask for feedback from Mr. Bruton and Mrs. Westman.

☐ I will share this portion or a more developed story with other adults including young adult author Dan Gemeinhart.

☐ Mr. Bruton will connect with my seventh-grade ELA teacher to let him or her know the progress made this year and the types of writing extensions that worked well.

Evidence of genuine
student–teacher
relationship

opportunities to engage in learning, students feel respected in the learning process *and learn.*

We need to create conditions for collaborative learning rather than group work.

We need to create conditions for collaborative learning rather than group work. This may seem like a lesson in semantics, but it is much more than that. In fact, group work without appropriate structure has the lowest effect on student achievement as compared to direct instruction or true cooperative learning (Kagan, 2013). To ensure all students in a group benefit from learning activities, all group members must have equal and active participation and opportunities to learn—the time-keeper does not have the same learning opportunity as the discussion leader.

There are multiple ways you can encourage true cooperative learning. Hattie recommends jig-sawing content amongst groups to be shared later.

Another way to ensure true cooperative learning is to provide structured ways for groups to run, like Kagan Structures. Kagan

Collaborative Learning Reminders

• Mix of ability, academic, and social-emotional strengths

• Highlight individual group member strengths.

• Groups are always fluid and flexible.

Teacher Voice

Cathy Boland, Eighth-Grade Science Teacher

Skokie School District

Skokie, IL

I had heard a great deal about Kagan Structures in my district but had yet to find the time to learn about them and implement them into my units. Up until then, my students and I were muddling through group work, but the results were sometimes disappointing. The stronger voices in the classroom often overtook the room, whereas the quieter voices hung back and sank into the background. Furthermore, I would become frustrated at the end of a unit when I noted the number of students who required reteaching.

I decided to schedule some time to work with our coach, Lisa Westman, so that I could not only learn about some fresh ideas, but that I could also co-teach with her and learn how best to use Kagan structures in the classroom. Lisa taught me two different structures, Round Robin and Rally Coach, that I could implement with my students:

Round Robin: Students take turns responding orally in their teams.

Rally Coach: In pairs, partner A solves the problem, while Partner B coaches, checks the accuracy of the answer and praises. Then, partners switch roles (Kagan, 2013).

We worked together to structure the strategies so that they would fit my students and unit in the best way possible so that I felt confident and also that my students could be successful.

Lisa modeled the approach for me and gradually released the teaching to me as the day went on until I was independent. I continued to use the strategies in a variety of ways, and it was quite successful! Not only were my students all equally engaged in learning, but the percentage of students requiring reteaching at the end of the unit shrunk dramatically—from 40% to less than 1%!

Structures are sets of consistently implemented simple structures to promote true cooperative learning, which are designed to work in any grade level or content area. Kagan Structures prescribe different structures for different types of learning activities and allow students to be easily grouped and regrouped heterogeneously with appropriately differentiated content and/ or tasks, depending academic and affective need (Kagan, 2013).

In the end, conscientious planning: collaboratively defining learning intentions and success criteria, offering students authentic and relevant learning hooks, determining how to use formative assessment data to inform instruction, differentiate and offer feedback, and strategically grouping students all help ensure the learning conditions are optimal for student success. However, without the most critical piece, student voice, all the planning in the world may prove to be fruitless.

Discussion Questions

▶ What role does an authentic hook play in planning learning opportunities?

▶ What are the learning intentions and success criteria, and why are they important?

▶ What is the most important component of formative assessment?

▶ How can feedback be used to differentiate instruction?

▶ What are important considerations when structuring cooperative learning and group-work opportunities?

Visit the companion website at http://resources.corwin .com/studentdrivendifferentiation.

Chapter 5

Include Student Voice

"A goal without a plan is just a wish."

—Antoine de Saint-Exupéry

Step 5: Set a Goal

What is the best way to promote student ownership? Engage in **goal setting**. Unfortunately, goal setting is often misunderstood. Sometimes people believe a goal must contain a number (I will get a 90% or above), or they set the goal too high (I will read 20 books this year), or use ambiguous language (I will pay attention every day in class).

Goal setting can be quite simple and a clear and relevant way to differentiate for students, while simultaneously promoting their ownership of the learning process.

Goals are personal. You cannot give someone a goal and expect him to "own" it.

Goals are personal. You cannot give someone a goal and expect him to "own" it. Rather, collaborate with students on goal setting. First, set the context and ensure that there is a common understanding of the learning intentions, success criteria, and what a quality goal looks like.

The most attainable goals are goals that are feasible, measurable, and sustainable. By measurable, I am referring to a way for the student to determine if she is meeting the goal, not a number on a test. Students would amaze me by setting super creative goals. For instance, one student set a vocabulary acquisition goal for herself. This student was going to "acquire vocabulary" by keeping a dictionary in her bathroom. Every morning when she brushed her teeth, she taught herself one new word. Then, she used this new word in class later that day (orally or in written form). This student never missed one day. Furthermore, when I planned instruction, I had information to better tailor group work to offer and monitor opportunities for this student to grow in her goal area as well as the other skills and standards assessed. You can read more about goal setting in Chapter 7 under the subheading, "Make Student Ownership Part of the Classroom Culture."

Step 6: Differentiate

Once you have formative assessment data and provide students with this information via feedback, it is likely that your conversations and interactions with the students will provide you with information as to which category(s) of differentiation are appropriate to adjust for the student's needs.

In my work with teachers on student-driven differentiation, I have encountered concerns about this step of student-driven differentiation. The three most common concerns have been:

▶ Not having enough time (*We have so much content to get through, it doesn't leave time for talking with students.*)

▶ The number of students they have (*I have too many students to talk to all of them on a regular basis.*)

▶ It feels uncomfortable to talk to students about their academic and/or social emotional needs.

In *Student Voice: The Instrument of Change* (2014), Russell Quaglia and Michael Corso address the first two of these three perceived barriers to which they respond with the following statements:

▶ Time sacrificed in the short run to listen to students pays off in the long run in the form of higher engagement. (p. 26)

▶ It is impossible to teach well without knowing your students. (p. 53)

Considering the third concern, talking with students about their needs, it is ok to feel uncomfortable about this. Historically, taking student voice into consideration has not been a component of teaching and learning. Therefore, using student voice to guide instruction may not come naturally, and you may have questions like those listed below.

Question: *What types of questions should I ask my students that will help drive instruction and differentiation?*

Suggestion: As educators, we often overthink things. Determining what questions to ask students to determine what they need to achieve in school is an example of overthinking. In short, to effectively use student voice to drive differentiation, ask questions related to the four categories of differentiation and then act accordingly. For example:

▶ *Content:* What intrigues you about this concept/topic? Or, for a student who is apathetic. Why do you find this content boring?

▶ *Process:* Is taking notes helping you to understand the material? If so, how do you know? If not, what learning strategy might be more helpful?

▶ *Product:* In an ideal world where you could show your understanding of this concept/topic in any way, how would you show it?

▶ *Learning environment:* Are you and your groupmates able to work collaboratively on this task? If so, how do you know? If not, what are your groups' obstacles?

> Listening to students relay information about their wants and needs does not necessarily mean you *do* whatever is asked. Listening means student thoughts are considered.

Question: *Will students become entitled if I do whatever they want?*

Suggestion: Listening to students relay information about their wants and needs does not necessarily mean you *do* whatever is asked. Listening means student thoughts are considered. Ask questions of students, summarize their responses to check for understanding, and then genuinely consider their questions/thoughts in relationship to your expectations. In doing so, you will gain information as to how to differentiate for their needs within the realm of your expectations.

Example

Teacher check-in with student: "It appears that you haven't made any progress on your PowerPoint."

Student response: "Can I make an infographic instead of a PowerPoint to present this information?"

Teacher response: "It sounds to me like you would like to present information about (state concept) in an infographic rather than a PowerPoint. Can you tell me how you will (state learning intentions) in an infographic?"

Teacher's next steps: Continue to converse with the student to continue to determine the best way the student can incorporate the learning intentions into his alternate product suggestion. If along the way it becomes clear that the suggested alternative won't allow the student to show understanding, converse with the student as to the reasons why; the student will likely have already come to the same conclusion.

Question: *How do I maintain boundaries with students? I am their teacher, not their friend.*

Suggestion: Be professional yet friendly and inviting when you talk with students. We have lots of conversations with people with whom we aren't trying to become friends; why are students any different? Follow the three tenets of building genuine relationships with students through conversation as outlined in Chapter 1: be real, be consistent, be a listener.

Step 7: Monitor Progress

Student-driven differentiation is most effective for students and most attainable by teachers when students set goals and monitor progress toward their goals (using formative assessment evidence), and teachers offer feedback in relation to the learning intentions, success criteria, and the students' goals. Students must know what they are learning, what it will look like when they get there, and where they are going next (Hattie, 2012). With these pieces clarified, students can monitor their growth and are likely to grow more than without these steps.

You can read more about student monitoring progress in Chapter 7.

Step 8: Assess Again

Assess again and determine effectiveness. Students will either show growth, and you can keep going, or students won't show growth, and you need to go back to Step 6, review the goal, either abandon or modify the goal, and then determine which learning strategies to try next to achieve the goal.

Figure 5.1   Ways Students Can Monitor Their Growth Toward Goals

Digital portfolio	On paper	Using a spreadsheet
Using video reflections	In a blog	Making an infographic

Figure 5.2   Planning Student-Driven Differentiation Graphic Organizer

Unit of Study/Lesson Name: _____

Standard and/or learning intentions:

Success criteria:

Hook:

Formative assessment notes:

Grouping notes:	Student goal-setting notes:

General student-driven differentiation notes, thoughts, and reflections:

Discussion Questions

▶ Why is it critical to plan student-driven learning experiences collaboratively?

▶ What role do goal setting and feedback play in informing student-driven differentiation?

▶ How can you include student voice in determining what and how students' needs can be met through differentiation?

▶ What perceived obstacles do you see? How might you overcome these obstacles?

Visit the companion website at http://resources.corwin .com/studentdrivendifferentiation.

Chapter 6

Student-Driven Differentiation Through Experiential Learning

I have been told that my greatest legacy in education will be the seventh- and eighth-grade *Shark Tank* (Burnett, 2009–2017) simulation I facilitated in 2014, which included a 45-minute student Q&A Skype session with real "shark," Mark Cuban. Truth be told, I hope *Shark Tank* is just one example of my mission to ensure all students have access to authentic and relevant learning opportunities.

You will notice I refer to *Shark Tank* as an authentic learning experience, whereas others will sometimes refer to the experience as *project-based learning* (PBL). Authentic learning and PBL can be synonymous if certain elements are present. In *High Impact Instruction* (2013), Jim Knight clearly explains these elements:

> Project-based learning is authentic so long as the emphasis of the project is on "authenticity" rather than the project itself. To be authentic learning, then, PBL has to:
>
> ▶ address a real-world issue
>
> ▶ produce a real-world product that addresses the issue

▶ be assessed using real-world criteria

▶ really engage the students

because they find the project interesting, meaningful, and personally relevant. (Knight, 2013, p. 227)

I have found that the most effective way to provide differentiated, high-interest learning options for students is to plan relevant, authentic experiences. These learning experiences need to

▶ account for pacing differences

▶ embed learning paths for groups of students

▶ allow for student autonomy (flexibility with structure)

Learning experiences with these criteria will result in significant student achievement and engagement.

This chapter shares several examples of ways other teachers and I have used authentic learning in our classrooms to create student-driven differentiated learning opportunities. They present success criteria that you can model to design student-driven differentiation in your classroom.

The next few sections will give you some practical approaches for using student voice to differentiate the learning environment. These examples are not meant to be prescriptive. These are applications that worked for me. They may not work for you. I strongly encourage you to create your own learning experiences for students by keeping in mind the eight-steps road map for student-driven differentiation.

As a reminder, those eight steps are

1. Define learning intentions and success criteria with your grade-level and/or department colleagues.

2. Hook the students to promote authentic engagement.

3. Assess students formatively and analyze results.

4. Group students and choose instructional strategies.

5. Set a goal with students.

6. Differentiate the content, process, product, and/or learning environment.

7. Monitor progress toward goal collaboratively.

8. Assess again to determine effectiveness.

Student-Driven Differentiation Example 1: Shark Tank

During the summer of 2014, I intertwined planning for the next school year with watching reruns of the reality TV show *Shark Tank*. I was continually struck by the addictive nature of the show and was surprised by how much I was learning about the business world.

As an adult, I had several questions and wondered if my students were asking themselves the same things: How do you arrive at the valuation for a company? What are the advantages of wholesale versus retail versus direct-to-consumer? What do proprietary and perpetuity mean? I started to envision an informational text unit for my seventh-grade English Arts students.

Content

To determine the validity of the idea, my colleague, Sara Denaro, and I focused on designing a project that allowed students to move through three phases of skills-based learning in the categories of Phase I: Reading, Phase II: Writing, Phase III: Speaking (see Figure 6.4). The phases allowed students to progress through the learning intentions at their pace and to varying levels of depth. The goal was to create original business ideas and pitch the business plans to real "sharks" in the Chicagoland area. Academic vocabulary was pulled from Season 5 of the show.

> **Reminder:** Most of the time, you will differentiate in more than one of the four categories of differentiation. You can see how categories were addressed with the *Shark Tank* simulation.

Our district had just adopted a new textbook series for English Language Arts (ELA). This was the core curriculum that all students received. The majority of our department was upset by this addition. While we understood the need for a common curriculum, we worried about losing autonomy and, in turn, losing our students' interest.

Sara and I had many of the same worries. But rather than looking at the textbook as an obstacle, we looked at it as a guide. Our first step was to align this *Shark Tank* idea with the prioritized standards identified for our informational text unit. Then, we collaborated to clearly and explicitly identify learning intentions and ensured we had a common understanding of the learning progressions and success criteria as indicated in Figure 6.4.

To hook students, we had them watch pitches of the show and analyze the content. These also served as examples of success criteria for Phase III: speaking of the

> **Why Three Phases of Learning?**
>
> Because there were three phases of the project, it was easier to adjust the pacing of the learning intentions for student's needs. In addition, they could move on to the next phase when they were ready and stay in a particular phase longer if they needed additional time to master the skills assessed in that phase.

project. We used a gradual release model of support to have students watch the clips and do the items indicated in Figures 6.1, 6.2, and 6.3. One of the unexpected advantages was that students became so "hooked" that they would go home and stream additional clips of *Shark Tank* to have more data to support what worked and what didn't work when giving pitches.

Figure 6.1   Gradual Release of Hook

1. Watch teacher-selected clips of pitches whole class. (I do.)

2. Watch clips of pitches whole class. Teacher prompts students with questions, and they "turn and talk" with a partner. Then some partner groups shared with the whole class. (I do; we do.)

3. Students watched clips of pitches both whole class and individually and scored them according to a rubric that *they created.* Additionally, students selected their own clips to share with the class. (You do.)

Figure 6.2   Teacher-Created Questions for Analyzing Clips
            (Project Hook)

1. How much is the initial asked investment?

2. How much is the equity stake?

3. What is the name of the business?

4. Did the pitch offer background information? If so, what information was provided?

5. What is their product or service?

6. What "problem" does this product/service alleviate?

7. What do they plan to do with the investment money?

8. Do the sharks invest?   Yes   No

9. Why, or why not?

10. Which shark invested?

11. What help can the investing shark provide (marketing, merchandising, technology support)?

Figure 6.3   Student-Created Scoring Rubric for Analyzing Clips
(Project Hook)

Question	Possible Points: 5—very clear and convincing 1—unclear and/or unconvincing
How the entrepreneur(s) pitched the idea	*/5*
How they marketed themselves and product/service	*/5*
How the entrepreneur(s) displayed confidence	*/5*
Whether the entrepreneur(s) had valid points about the potential success of their product/service	*/5*
What the entrepreneur(s) should do with their investment money	*/5*
Whether you agree with the sharks	*/5*
EXTRA: **Explanation of other details about the pitch that you feel are important**	**Notes**

Figure 6.4   Differentiating Content, Process, Product, and Learning Environment

Standards Assessed	Learning Intentions	Success Criteria
Phase I: Reading CCSS.ELA-Literacy.RI.7.2 Determine two or more central ideas in a text and analyze their development over the course of the text; provide an objective summary of the text. CCSS.ELA-Literacy.RI.7.3 Analyze the interactions.	☐ Determine the central idea in a text. ☐ Analyze how the central idea permeates the text. ☐ Summarize text. ☐ Compare and contrast. **Guiding Questions** 1. *What makes one successful? Are there any commonalities between these people?*	Written response for each of the learning intentions (examples and non-examples were shared with students) prior to their presentations.

(Continued)

Figure 6.4   (Continued)

Standards Assessed	Learning Intentions	Success Criteria
between individuals, events, and ideas in a text (e.g., how ideas influence individuals or events, or how individuals influence ideas or events). Learning standards aligned to the textbook series we were using. We build upon the activities and formative assessments prescribed by the textbook.	2. *What distinguishes different industries? How do they compare and contrast?* 3. *What do you need to know about the industry you would like to start a business in?*	

How did student voice drive the differentiation for Phase I: Reading?

Content: Students were offered a variety of readings (different excerpts from each of the shark's biographies, different articles about the business industry, and the option to curate their own readings. They had autonomy to pick and choose the reading that most appealed to them.

Process:

1. Students had the option to choose from a variety of learning strategies to show their understanding of the readings and answer the questions listed above. They were able to choose using premade graphic organizers, creating their own mind maps, filming video reflections, or using a strategy of their own choosing.

2. We gave students feedback (both in person and digitally) regarding their understanding of the concepts and helped them determine next steps (i.e., *"You have selected two relevant texts about entrepreneurship in the tech space. I can clearly see both experts' perspectives with the text evidence you state. Now, determine which perspective would be most helpful to you as you write your business plan and why. Then, share your next steps for additional feedback."*).

3. Students monitored their own progress toward learning intentions using a digital monitoring guide.

Phase II: Writing	☐ Introduce a topic and organize	A business plan
CCSS.ELA-Literacy.W.7.2 Write informative/explanatory texts to examine a topic and convey ideas, concepts, and information through the selection, organization, and analysis of relevant content.	ideas, concepts, and information to make important connections and distinctions; include formatting (e.g., headings), graphics (e.g., figures, tables), and multimedia when useful to aiding comprehension.	which identifies each of the learning intentions (which were a separate formative assessment) and houses them all together

Standards Assessed	Learning Intentions	Success Criteria
CCSS.ELA-Literacy.W.7.4 Produce clear and coherent writing in which the development, organization, and style are appropriate to task, purpose, and audience.	☐ Develop the topic with well-chosen, relevant, and sufficient facts, extended definitions, concrete details, quotations, or other information and examples appropriate to the audience's knowledge of the topic. ☐ Use precise language and domain-specific vocabulary. ☐ Demonstrate understanding of connotation and denotation of words and the effect of communication.	

How did student voice drive the differentiation for Phase II: Writing?

Content: Students had complete autonomy as to the business/product they would create. This vision drove their research process, and students were responsible for determining what resources they needed, and teachers helped students solicit the information they needed.

Process: Students were flexibly grouped initially by industry (technology, food services, textiles, etc.) to make the research process more efficient as students could conquer and share pertinent information. As students progressed through their research and started writing their business plans (template was provided as suggested areas to include, but no parts were mandated), they were regrouped to work with students who were working at the same pace to offer each other peer feedback.

Product: A template was provided for students to follow as a form of scaffolding if needed. Student business plans differed as many students chose to infuse their personalities into their business plans. The level of sophistication in the business plans was outstanding and exceeded our expectations.

Phase III: Speaking CCSS.ELA-Literacy.SL.7.4 Present claims and findings, emphasizing salient points in a focused, coherent manner with pertinent descriptions, facts, details, and examples; use appropriate eye contact, adequate volume, and clear pronunciation.	☐ Come to discussions prepared, having read or researched material under study; explicitly draw on that preparation by referring to evidence on the topic. ☐ Follow rules for collegial discussions, monitor progress toward specific goals and deadlines, and define individual roles as needed.	Each learning intention was assessed formatively for mastery, and then all learning intentions were presented together as a "business pitch." Pitches were presented to students

(Continued)

Figure 6.4   (Continued)

Standards Assessed	Learning Intentions	Success Criteria
CCSS.ELA-Literacy. SL.7.5 Include multimedia components and visual displays in presentations to clarify claims and findings and emphasize salient points.	☐ Pose questions that elicit elaboration and respond to others' questions and comments with relevant observations and ideas that bring the discussion back on topic as needed. ☐ Acknowledge new information expressed by others (in the form of questions from sharks/teachers/ students), and when warranted, modify their own views.	and teachers. Finalists presented to real "sharks" and needed to be prepared to answer questions about your business/ product.

How did student voice drive the differentiation for Phase III: Speaking?

Product: Similar to Phase II: Writing, the students had complete autonomy as to how they would best pitch their product and/or company. Using the information, they learned from analyzing clips from the show the final pitches all took on different forms. Some groups had interactive pitches (they gave samples for judges to try, some created working prototypes including an app for an iPhone). Other groups demonstrated their creativity with things like rapping part of their pitch, and other groups gave more traditional pitches that were loaded with information.

Students all pitched their ideas for a group of their peers and a group of teachers.

All of the students prepared to answer anticipated questions from sharks, which encouraged a higher level of thinking. The feedback students received encouraged many of the finalist groups to adjust their pitches to proactively address questions they had been asked.

Vocabulary	capital	proprietary
(word list compiled from Season 5 of *Shark Tank*)	consignment	provisional
	differentiate	retail
	direct-to-consumer	royalty
	entrepreneur	trademark
	franchise	ubiquitous
	industry	utility
	marketing	valuation
	patent	venture capital
	perpetuity	wholesale
	pitch	

How did student voice drive the differentiation for vocabulary instruction?

A variety of instructional strategies were used to help students gain an understanding of the vocabulary words for the unit. Twitter, Instagram, and the use of hashtags were gaining popularity. Students decided they wanted to create a "classroom feed" of hashtags for the vocabulary so they created a word wall on colored sheets of papers. As students felt they understood the meaning of a word, they would add a hashtag to the sheet of paper. For example, the word *wholesale* was hashtagged #gobigorgohome.

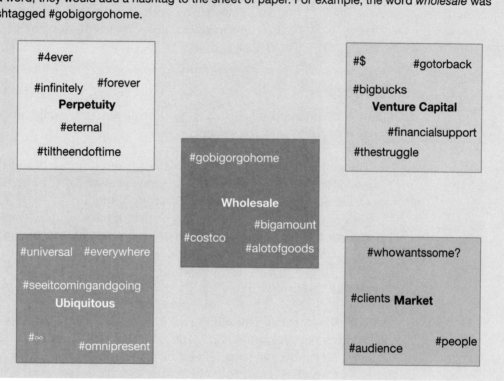

Source: Learning intentions adapted from California Common Core Standards Learning Progression Guide, www.commoncore.tcoe.org

For two-thirds of this simulation students chose the content they would read to demonstrate mastery of the skills and learning standards. Our role was not to impart knowledge, but rather to guide students through the learning progressions at their own pace. Having three phases allowed us to do this seamlessly, while building students' collective capacity to guide each other.

Common Question: *How will I keep students on track if they are all learning different content?*

Answer: Make the learning intentions about the skill. Offer students feedback on the process, and next steps rather than content in and of itself.

Offering students differentiated feedback was vital to the success of this learning model. We did not need to know all of the content, but we did need to understand where the students were on the learning progression. By knowing the learning progressions, we could easily ascertain whether or not students were comprehending the content or not and adapt our instruction as needed. We focused on the process, in other words, how the students would learn the content.

Process

Effective differentiation, including student-driven differentiation, relies largely on flexibly grouping students.

> The grouping aspect [of differentiation] is often not well understood. The aim is not necessarily to group students by their phase of learning, etc., but rather to group by a mixture of those +1 above, so that peer mediation can be part of moving all forward. Having students both at or +1 above the phase of learning can help students move forward as they discuss with, work together with, and see the world through the eyes of the other students. (Hattie, 2011, p. 110)

Therefore, for Phase I: Reading of the project, my colleague and I grouped the students heterogeneously and targeted reading skills using a variety of readings. We jigsawed all required reading material by breaking up an article into four parts or assigning four different articles for the group members to read and share, thereby ensuring that each member of the group had the same level of work.

A fortuitous outcome of these initial groupings was students learned more about their classmates' interests, views on business, and goals, which later helped them choose business partners based on goals rather than allegiances.

During Phase II: Writing and Phase III: Speaking, students largely worked in pairs rather than small groups. However, we still continued to employ flexible grouping. We modeled what group discussions should look like and were impressed with how quickly the students started giving each other actionable feedback.

One of my favorite examples of this was during the beginning of Phase II: the research and writing phase of the project as student groups were researching market demand for their ideas as indicated in Figure 6.5.

Figure 6.5   Example Student Discussion

Student 1:	"Oh, no. Our business idea already exists."
Student 2:	"Did you know that already?"
Student 1:	"No. I just found out with my Google search."
Student 2:	"Have you ever heard of the competitor?"
Student 1:	"No."
Student 2:	"Well, I think that's actually a good thing. That shows there is a market demand, but the company isn't reaching the market. Now, you can focus on what they *aren't* doing and dominate the market."
Student 1:	"Totally! I think we need to survey potential buyers to see what they want. Thank you for the guidance."

Product

One of the products students completed was formulating high-level, text-based questions to ask Mark Cuban during a Skype Q&A. Students drafted their questions along with an explanation of how the answer to their questions would aid the development of their businesses. Figure 6.6 is a sampling of the questions that were asked during the Q&A:

For Phase III: Speaking, students delivered business pitches.

Students created a rubric influenced by the article *The Successful 'Shark Tank' Pitch: Mark Cuban's 7 Tips* (Valiente, 2013). Students used their rubric to assess the Shark Tank pitches they viewed online. This exercise engaged students and provided them with concrete examples of what they needed to do (and not do) to ensure they got an offer from a shark.

Common Concern: *ELA lends itself to projects. Math does not.*

Solution: All content areas have real-life applications. Create context for math units.

Learning Environment

We used Skype to differentiate the learning environment. Students were able to connect with experts in their industry (food services, EdTech, Fashion, etc.) to gather information and to receive feedback on progress. We refurbished a large closet in our classroom and made a soundproof "office." We used QuickTime to record Skype sessions so students could go back and rewatch their sessions and share with their parents and classmates to solicit feedback.

Students often traveled to visit other teachers in our building for further guidance. Some students met with math teachers to help them set

Figure 6.6　Student Questions for Mark Cuban

- In your book, *How to Win at the Sport of Business,* you said, "People will always take the path of the least resistance." I agree with that sentiment, but it appears that, as a businessman, you are not tempted by the easy way out. What advice do you have for young entrepreneurs to avoid taking the path of least resistance, for example: watching TV instead of reading?

- In your book, you referred to investors as people that steal your company and destiny, and care about nothing other than money. You are an investor on *Shark Tank,* do you view yourself differently?

- In class, we read an article published in *Forbes Magazine* last June. We discovered that *Shark Tank* requires show participants to give up 5% of their company or a 2% royalty just for appearing on the show regardless of whether or not they get a deal. The article offered two viewpoints, one positive and one negative. What do you think of this policy?

- In an interview with ABC News, you gave seven tips on how to make a successful pitch. You listed factors that make a good, solid presentation. What kind of pitch do you find most effective? (Comical, heartfelt, straightforward?)

- In your book *How to Win at the Sport of Business,* you have a chapter titled "Connecting to Customers" in which you say, "treat your customers like they own you because, they do." Based on your extensive knowledge on businesses, what is the most important: the investor, the customers, or the employees, and why?

- In your book you say that after your business has been validated, and you've confirmed there is a big market for your business and you've gotten lots of good advice, raising cash is the next step that many people take. You say that taking that step is a big mistake. Can you elaborate on this please?

valuations for their companies, determine their margins, and ascertain customer acquisition costs. Some students worked with our science and art teachers to help them design and build working prototypes of products.

Seventh-grade students pitched their business ideas to eighth-grade students, and eighth-grade pitched to seventh-grade students. Student observers used the rubric they created to assess their peers. Student observers played the part of sharks by asking probing questions of the student presenters.

Ultimately, the 12 student partnerships with the highest scores (as assessed by their peers) pitched their business ideas to a panel of Chicagoland sharks during an evening event that was open to the community. The sharks treated the students as adults and asked them the same level of questions they would ask an actual prospective investment candidate. Students in the audience (and Sara and I) were stumped by some of the questions and were proud to see our student presenters using strategies they had practiced in class discussions to engage in meaningful conversations with the visiting panel.

Now, 3 years later, two of our student business ideas have been realized by other entrepreneurs. Our "Got A Ride?" idea (an Uber service for kids) is up and running in Los Angeles as HopSkipDrive and our student business

"GoKart" (a Bluetooth shopping experience) has been actualized by Amazon in their new Amazon Go Stores.

For an adaptation of this *Shark Tank* authentic learning opportunity for elementary-aged students, please see the "invention convention" example in Chapter 8.

Student-Driven Differentiation Example 2: Mock Trial

Role playing is a natural behavior that children and adults alike use to learn (think playing "house" as children or dressing up for Halloween at any age). Tapping into this inclination is a great way to make learning authentic for students. Student participation in a mock trial is one example of how to implement this in a classroom setting.

My favorite mock trial curriculum comes from Minnesota Center for Community Legal Education (www.teachingcivics.org). There are many free quality options available online. Students can also create their own trial based on historical events, current events, and so on.

Standard assessed—SS.IS.5.6-8.MdC

☐   Identify evidence from multiple sources to support claims, noting its limitations.

Drawing by Eighth-Grade Mock Trial Participant

Courtesy of Ethan Dan

☐ Construct explanations using reasoning, correct sequence, examples, and details, while acknowledging their strengths and weaknesses.

☐ Compare the means by which individuals and groups change societies, promote the common good, and protect rights.

Learning Intentions: Make a claim, support a claim with evidence, and consider and address a counterargument to claim using domain-specific (legal) vocabulary.

Success Criteria: Students (orally and/or in written form) demonstrate their ability to logically analyze and critique a claim and evidence.

Hook: Video clips of courtroom scenes from *Legally Blond* (Luketic, 2001) and *Bee Movie* (Smith, Hickner, & Seinfeld, 2007)

Research-based high impact instructional strategies used: Feedback, gradation of skills, cooperative learning, choice, flexible grouping, and flexible pacing based on evidence from formative assessment.

Mock Trial Gradation of Skills

Based on pre-assessment data, students are assigned a role that aligns to their skill level and provided appropriate scaffolds or challenges to support student learning (Figure 6.7).

Materials: Mock Trial Manual from the Minnesota Center for Community Legal Education at www.teachingcivics.org

▶ All: Courtroom procedures, domain specific vocabulary

▶ Lawyers: Court case (both prosecution and defense packets)

▶ Witnesses: Court case (only side student represents)

▶ Jurors: Current event articles about court cases

Figure 6.7   Mock Trial Gradation of Skills

Jurors	Witnesses	Attorneys
Less complex: evaluate an argument	**Meets success criteria:** state a claim and support with evidence	**More complex:** make and support a claim with evidence; address counter-argument

Student Voice Component: Students complete a personality or strengths assessment (we used Thrively for our strengths assessment, but you can use a variety of online options or create your own that helps them identify their strengths—i.e., public speaking, analytical, creative) and also rank their preference of roles in the mock trial. All students received their first or second choice (see Figure 6.8).

Figure 6.8   Sample Role Choice Form

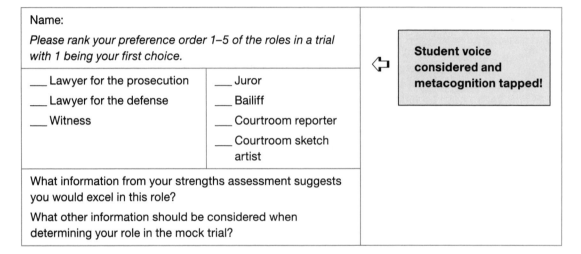

Name:

Please rank your preference order 1–5 of the roles in a trial with 1 being your first choice.

___ Lawyer for the prosecution	___ Juror
___ Lawyer for the defense	___ Bailiff
___ Witness	___ Courtroom reporter
	___ Courtroom sketch artist

What information from your strengths assessment suggests you would excel in this role?

What other information should be considered when determining your role in the mock trial?

⇦ **Student voice considered and metacognition tapped!**

Student-Driven Differentiation Example 3: The Amazing Geography Race

As an instructional coach, I love partnering with teachers and watching them achieve their student-driven differentiation goals. Carrie Eccleston was the first teacher I worked with as an instructional coach and one of the most rewarding experiences I had partnering with someone using the model of student-driven differentiation.

Carrie had taught social studies for many years when she came to talk to me about a goal she had for teaching her students. Carrie relayed that although she taught geography concepts like longitude and latitude and students showed mastery of these concepts, she couldn't help but feel bothered by the fact that students shared feedback with her that they didn't see how the content related to them or why it was important to know.

Additionally, our district had just gone 1:1, and Carrie and her students expressed an interest to better utilize their new Chromebooks. Read Carrie's account of how she incorporated her students' collective voice to create an authentic, student-driven differentiated learning experience that expanded the walls of the classroom for her students.

Teacher Voice

Carrie Eccleston, Sixth-Grade Social Studies Teacher

Skokie School District 73.5

Skokie, IL

In the Fall of 2015, my grade-level department colleague and I set a goal for ourselves to analyze my current geography assessments to better align with the standards we were assessing and also to provide an opportunity for students to authentically invest in learning. The test we were working with was 10 years old and had been tweaked over the years to address different skills that we were teaching. Each of the skills, however, was tested in isolation. Students were asked to locate places using latitude and longitude, identify landforms in the United States, and define vocabulary words. This was where the breakdown appeared to be: The students couldn't connect these skills to an outside context. I was frustrated with the drill and kill feeling of the test and wanted to upgrade it to something where the students would *use* the skills to solve a problem and connect to the real world. We also wanted an assessment that all students could access. So often fun and creative projects are saved for "extensions" in the learning. I believe that all students should have access to these creative assessments.

My colleague and I worked with our differentiation coach (Lisa) on our goals for the assessment. The standard we were addressing was: *Use geographic representations (maps, photographs, satellite images, etc.) to explain the relationships between the locations (places and regions) and changes in their environment.* After throwing around some different ideas, Lisa said she would do some research and bring some of her findings back to us so we could think about them together.

The very next day, Lisa came back with a thinking prompt, which was a game based on *The Amazing Race* she found on a website. We loved the concept but were still trying to figure out *how to have the students practice their geography skills and apply their knowledge to explain the relationships between the locations and the changes in the environment.* Plus, we felt like there was more we could do to offer students ownership in the game. I was fixated on genuinely connecting it to the real world.

After much discussion, I thought of something that might connect with our students and resonate with the world around us: What if we put out a message to our friends on Facebook and asked them to record a short video of themselves somewhere in the world? We could ask them to give clues as to where they were, emphasizing the natural features of an area as well as highlight manmade cultural landmarks. We also asked them to offer up clues such as the latitude and longitude of the location, or the continent they were on, but not say exactly where they were. The three of us posted the request. Within 2 weeks, we had 20 short videos from many different parts of the United States as well as Europe, Africa, Asia, Australia, and New Zealand. It was incredible!

Naturally, some videos were short, others were longer, some were from very obscure locations in Africa, and others were from more obvious places in the United States. Some of our volunteers gave very tangible clues, and other people's clues were more obscure. We loved the videos and once we had them, our work was not done. Instead, we looked to differentiate the assessment.

Our goal was to provide a fun and engaging way for students to work together to use their geography skills to successfully locate different places in the world and make connections between the location and changes in their environment. We decided to structure the game by calling it The Amazing Geography Race. We organized the videos into four different "levels" based on location familiarity, content of the message, and length. We then created a generic "Passport" that each team could use. Each team had to listen to a set of videos, take notes to gather clues, and then *use their atlas, an online encyclopedia, and their geography skills* to find out the location of the person in the video. Once they identified the location, they had to answer additional questions about the specific natural or cultural features in that area. This prompted students *to explain the relationship between the location and changes in the environment.*

Because some videos were simpler than others, we were able to set up four leveled teams that had five clues each. They completed the same tasks, practiced the same skills, and made connections between relationships using differentiated clues (content). Each group was working at their own level, and yet they were all practicing the same skills meeting the same standard (use geographic representations [maps, photographs, satellite images, etc.] to explain the relationships between the locations [places and regions] and changes in their environment).

Watching the students meet the standard equitably was so eye opening. Each team was challenged, had fun, competed against each other, and learned about the world around them. There were people in Alaska teaching the students about the effects of climate change on the glaciers, and people in New Zealand sharing information about earthquakes. There were students in China who featured a famous tea house and a family in California who taught the students about the drought.

Setting up this project took a lot of thought, but now it is done. We have used it for the last 3 years, and we have tweaked it and changed it to make it better and more streamlined each time.

Setting up this project took a lot of thought, but now it is done. We have used it for the last 3 years, and we have tweaked it and changed it to make it better and more streamlined each time. In the past, I may have set

(Continued)

(Continued)

up one game for all students to play and organized the class into hetero-geneous groups. The more dominant students would have taken over, and the more passive ones would have watched and followed. Setting up four differentiated routes allowed all students to have access. Flexibly group-ing students based on formative assessment data allowed all students to access content and be engaged at their level.

Amazing Race Simulation

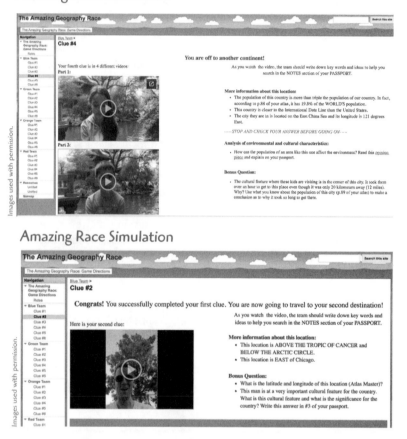

Amazing Race Simulation

Student-Driven Differentiation Example 4: Mock ER

Renee, middle school science teacher, turned K–8 inquiry specialist, turned Teaching and Learning Coordinator for Lake Forest School District 67 in Illinois, is a master at creating authentic, student-driven learning experi-ences for students.

I met Renee my first year teaching. She had started at the same school the year before me. At the end of that school year, Renee's students ran a mock ER with student doctors, nurses, and hospital staff, while teachers and administrators acted as patients. Renee asked me to be one of the patients. I found the experience to be eye-opening and inspirational. Students were working at their level to reach a shared goal: collaboratively diagnosis patients, offer a prognosis, and prescribe treatment. I credit Renee with showing me my first example of a success criteria for student-driven differentiation. In the following vignette, read about Renee's experience with the mock ER.

Teacher Voice

Renee Fitzsimmons, Eighth-Grade Science Teacher

Lake Forest School District 67

Lake Forest, IL

As a first-year teacher in 1997 tasked with teaching science to a group of eighth graders, I remember the fear in my soul as students entered the classroom. Questions flooded my mind. Was it just me or did some of these students appear to not want to be here? How would I control this classroom since most students were bigger than me? How would I teach nucleic acids and DNA when most students didn't even understand the concept of a molecule? How do I help the child asking when we would begin triangulating buildings so as to be able to start physics calculations when I don't even know what that means?

It goes without saying I was petrified about being able to make sense of what seemed to be irrelevant science standards in the eyes of most 14-year-olds. I also had to keep all students interested, maintain order and some semblance of classroom management, and accommodate the diverse needs in my classroom. I realized I had two choices. One was to follow the sample lessons that were passed down to me and have a really strong behavior management plan in place for when students were not engaged and off task. Should questions arise that I didn't know the answers to as a new teacher, I could fake knowing the answers and put the students off until they forgot or didn't care about their questions. My second choice was to figure out *why* anyone would need to understand these seemingly useless standards, frame all units under those pretexts, and be completely honest when I didn't know the answer to questions by saying, "I don't know, and I'm hoping you can help me find a way to discover the answer."

I always apologize to my first year of students when I bump into them, but thankfully, in my *second* year of teaching, I opted for choice number

(Continued)

(Continued)

two, and the result was complete chaos, intense coordination, a little improv, crazy frontloaded hard work, a ton of laughs and fun, and a lot of student learning.

Let me explain with a specific example. I began planning a life science unit by asking myself why anyone would need to learn about human biology standards, and my answer was simple: Everyone needs to learn about staying healthy. We took on the lens of the medical field, and I walked in one day saying we were applying to medical school. Students needed to fill out college applications to a school of medicine of their choice and interest (School of Cardiology, Pulmonary Medicine, Neurology, Intestinal Medicine, Immunology, etc.). Each "school" was charged with the task of learning everything they could about that particular body system by following a loose rubric containing necessary components to research, learn, and ultimately become the experts in order to teach others. While each group collaborated, I had the gift of time to work with individual students and teams to support them in the unique way they each needed.

We culminated with graduation into surgery (the dissection of the fetal pig) and finally our Residency in the ER (Emergency Room), which was a mock simulation where staff and parents surprised the students with mystery ailments (chosen specifically for their area of expertise) in return for a diagnosis and treatment plan. While this unit is dated and far from perfect, the anecdotal evidence has proven that *this type of learning supports organic differentiation and a way to "teach up" where all students are empowered, and therefore, learning is personalized.*

First, I learned that when I answered a student's question with, "I don't know, let's find out together," I expected them to look at me like I was a disappointment as their teacher, but instead, their sense of empowerment was what made them not only learn more than I could have ever taught them, but they actually felt good about being in my class. They felt they were helping me, while answering their own questions. I also learned that encouraging students to ask and seek answers to their own questions only solicited more questions and the desire to seek answers to those questions. Students' questions became the road map that drove our learning. As I became a more seasoned teacher and often times knew the answers to their questions, I continued to feign uncertainty.

> While I have always taught so that standards framed our learning, students never knew that I was secretly guiding their learning journey like the guardrails on a highway.

While I have always taught so that standards framed our learning, students never knew that I was secretly guiding their learning journey like the guardrails on a highway. I learned I had a gift for improvisation and was able to make students feel their questions were driving the daily work, even though I had backwards designed the unit and knew our final destination. I find this takes some of the fear out of the myth that student-driven learning is unrelated to standards or completely unfocused. That is not to say that often times our journey took a detour based on where students wanted to go, but it took many years to develop a sense of confidence in the facilitation of student-led conversations, solicitation of the right questions, and creation of student-designed experiments and research to test their theories.

Second, engagement and behavior management was never an issue because students were empowered. Each day of learning had purpose and meaning framed by an essential and challenge question responsible for propelling our work together. Our mock ER was evidence of this as you would never know, it was the last academic day of school for graduating eighth graders whose grades had already been turned in, yet they were still intensely rushing around the multipurpose room dressed like surgeons, calling out different codes and working like a team to save our patients. Students were past simply being compliant. They were even beyond engaged. They were empowered. Empowered students driving their own learning have the necessary skills for receiving their driver's permit to enter the *Age of Innovation* that is on the horizon.

Third, differentiation became an organic and natural part of our learning environment. The work we were doing in science was high level. By "teaching up" with purposeful and meaningful learning focused on student voice and choice, learning is deeper at whatever level is appropriate for that student because they will take it to that level themselves. It will be individualized and will meet their unique needs because *they* are curious and passionate. For instance, middle school physical science standards in chemistry require deep understanding of the conservation of matter and mass. By framing this unit with the understanding that chemistry has changed our lives and ultimately charging students to work for a biotech or pharmaceutical company, I was able to facilitate an understanding of purpose for learning this principle through seeing we can make new matter from old matter.

Today, I am a Teaching and Learning Coordinator for a school district in Illinois, and I have the profound pleasure of supporting teachers tweak their already amazing practices to include small changes like these that have had enormous impacts on differentiated student learning in all subjects. I encourage you to reflect on your own practices and find ways you can transform your classroom this year. Remember to always ask yourself two very simple questions when planning a single lesson or an entire unit:

1. Why would a student want or need to learn this content in order for it to be relevant to them or their future?

(Continued)

2. How can I make this learning authentic while including as much student voice and choice as possible?

In working with teachers today, the most common feedback I hear is that this type of teaching and learning at first pushes us outside of our comfort zone, and the work is exhausting, but the learning excitement and reward is like nothing else they have ever experienced. In the end, empowered learners are organically differentiated for, and their learning will be deeper and more personalized than we could have ever planned.

What Does This Mean for You?

Authentic learning experiences may not be right for every class. However, there are real-life applications for everything students learn. We can facilitate these learning opportunities by relying on the guide to student-driven differentiation and the checklist for planning "real-life" learning experiences (Figure 6.9).

Regardless of the learning opportunities you plan, an important final step in every unit is to earnestly reflect on the unit's success. I recommend using the Figure 6.10 Reflection Guide to reflect on (both individually and with your colleagues) and amend the unit as necessary for future use.

Figure 6.9   Checklist for Planning "Real-Life" Learning Experiences

☐   There are outside sources (people) we can tap into as resources.

☐   I can easily find examples of non-student created success criteria (i.e., a *Shark Tank* pitch).

☐   The simulation allows for students to take different roles.

☐   There are options that allow students to choose content.

☐   The success criteria are defined, yet the product type is flexible so students can determine how to best demonstrate the success criteria.

☐   The simulation promotes authentic engagement rather than compliance.

*I know this because: (list at least two ways authentic engagement is promoted)

1. _____

2. _____

3. _____

Figure 6.10 Reflection Guide

- Why did I ask students to complete this task?
- Did I accomplish my goal? How do I know?
- How did the phases of this task provide information about students' progress toward the success criterion?
- What do I need to do differently in the future?
- Did this simulation promote collaboration (student to student and student to teacher)? How do I know?
- Did this simulation promote student ownership? How do I know?
- Did this simulation consider student readiness appropriately?
- Did this simulation promote a positive rather than punitive learning community?
- What feedback have the students given me about this simulation?

Discussion Questions

▶ What does the phrase *flexibility within structure* mean to you?

▶ What role do the learning intentions and success criteria play in allowing you to strike a balance of flexibility within structure?

▶ What ideas do you have for creating student-driven differentiated learning experiences for your students?

▶ How can collaborating with other teachers or an instructional coach help you to create authentic student-driven, differentiated learning experiences?

Visit the companion website at http://resources.corwin .com/studentdrivendifferentiation.

Part III

Reimagining Schools

7

Create Learning Environments That Promote Student Ownership

"If I had asked people what they wanted, they would have said faster horses."

—(often attributed to) Henry Ford

Don't Update the Factory Model; Discard It Altogether

In the past 200+ years, there have only been a small handful of iterations in learning environments. Students who attended school in the 18th and early 19th centuries were educated in one-room school houses until the Industrial Revolution, and there was a need for larger schools and more efficient means of educating the students in those schools. School operating systems were modeled after factory operating systems, which were growing exponentially during this time. School switched from a one-room schoolhouse to class-rooms with very specific focuses (either grade level or content areas), and students were placed in rows to sit and learn from a teacher through direct instruction. The primary focus of school during this time was for teachers to impart knowledge and for students to demonstrate retention of knowledge.

For frame of reference, in 1900, the Model-T was introduced by Henry Ford, homes did not have refrigerators, child labor was still legal, and computer was a job title (one who computes), not a machine. Our world has changed, but comparably our learning environment has not. Rather than listing all the advances our world has experienced, I'll just mention one example of a reason our learning environment must change: Google. If our primary role as teachers is to impart knowledge, in today's world, we will lose to Google every time.

> If our primary role as teachers is to impart knowledge, in today's world, we will lose to Google every time.

Don't get me wrong, there is still a need for content knowledge, but in order to differentiate content, the process, or the product with students in the driver seat, we must first differentiate the learning environment. And, to differentiate the learning environment, we need to think about structures other than schools as we have known them.

In a 2017 blog post, I addressed the learning environment and explained how above all, failure to address this piece of our instruction is the reason differentiation fails so often. While the title of the post suggests the content pertains to gifted learners, the premise of the post pertains to the importance of differentiating the learning environment so that all students' needs are met in mixed-ability classrooms.

Why Differentiation Misses the Mark for Gifted Students

by Lisa Westman

April 20, 2017

Finding Common Ground blogs.edweek.org

Last week I wrote *Differentiation: Attainable or Somewhere Over the Rainbow* which addresses some common objections related to differentiated instruction—one of these arguments being that many educators and gifted education advocates believe the needs of gifted students are not being met in the "regular" classroom through differentiation.

Dr. Jim Delisle, author and gifted education expert, brought this topic to the forefront in his 2015 EdWeek Commentary Piece, *Differentiation Doesn't Work*. I remember initially feeling quite defensive when I read the article.

Delisle claims that differentiation is nothing more than a great proposition that is impossible to achieve: "It seems to me that the only educators who assert that differentiation is doable are those who have never tried to implement it themselves: university professors, curriculum coordinators, and school principals." He warns readers that it is our high-achieving students who stand to lose the most from the unfulfilled promise of differentiation. According to Delisle, there is only one possible solution to meet the needs of these students, "Differentiation might have a chance to work if we are willing, as a nation, to return to the days when students of similar abilities were placed in classes with other students whose learning needs paralleled their own."

Delisle is not entirely wrong.

If a teacher wants to differentiate effectively in a traditional classroom setting, I agree with Delisle when he says, "Although fine in theory, differentiation in practice is harder to implement in a heterogeneous classroom than it is to juggle with one arm tied behind your back."

Effectively differentiating instruction in a customary classroom setting (teacher imparts knowledge and students show they retain the information) is like trying to fit a square peg into a round hole. One teacher cannot conduct three different lectures simultaneously. When a teacher in a traditional classroom is presented with a class made up of all types of learners, they are forced to teach to the middle, which builds frustration for gifted and struggling students alike.

Therefore, I can understand when Delisle suggests reverting back to tracked classes, with students sorted neatly into groups of learners with similar abilities. All students deserve the opportunity to learn at a pace that is appropriate for them, and tracking students certainly does make pacing easier.

We are solving the wrong problem.

Now, before the gifted folks jump on me again, let me preface: As a former gifted teacher and a differentiation instructional coach, I am an ardent proponent of identifying gifted students just as we identify special education students. The needs of gifted students, without question, require special consideration, action plans, follow-through, and monitoring.

That being said, I also strongly believe that these students' needs can be met through differentiated instruction in a "regular" classroom—because differentiation itself is not the problem. Rather, our nation's lack of ubiquitous implementation of differentiated instruction is a symptom of a much larger problem.

The actual issue is the lingering remnants of the factory model and mindset still largely ingrained in our educational system today. Case in

(Continued)

(Continued)

point: Tracking students is a direct result of schools that prepared students for predetermined career paths.

During the industrialization era, students were placed on tracks with finite destinations: factory worker, tradesman, or professional with a higher-level degree. Future tradesmen sat next to other future tradesmen, future professionals learned alongside other future professionals.

But putting students on these same tracks today poses a significant problem because these tracks no longer lead to known destinations. As first indicated in a report from the US Department of Labor called *Future Work Trends and Challenges for Work in the 21st Century* (1999) and later analyzed for potential implications and solutions for schools by the International Society for Technology in Education (ISTE) Connects, 65% of jobs to become available in the future have yet to be created (Team ISTE, 2016).

Job trends since 1999 support this statistic as new jobs and categories in the services provided industry continue to experience exponential growth, while other industries like manufacturing, continue to trend downward (US Bureau of Labor Statistics, 2017).

With this information in mind, our focus must shift from preparing students to interact with similar learners to finding ways to ensure our students can productively collaborate with all types of learners. Doing so is critical for our students' long-term success.

Therefore, teachers must conduct orchestras, not trains.

If our ever-evolving world is not a compelling enough reason to focus on the real problem, let's also consider this: Even in a gifted or tracked class, teachers still need to differentiate for their students.

Programming alone will not meet students' needs. In *Beyond Gifted Education, Designing and Implementing Advanced Academic Programs* (2013), authors Scott Peters, Michael Matthews, Matthew McBee, and D. Betsy McCoach state, "Not all students who are labeled gifted require the same things in order to receive an appropriate educational experience. Just as not all gifted students require the same services, a given individual (gifted or not) does not automatically need the same services year after year" (p. 3).

The bottom line is—learners' needs, gifted or not, are fluid. Learning is fluid. However, our current educational system is largely static. We hear a lot of talk about student and teacher innovation. Many times we look to the silver bullet (as Peter DeWitt points out in *Can We Destroy the Silver Bullet Mentality Before it Destroys Us?*) which takes on the form of implementing a tech tool or making something fit in our current practice without changing what we have always done (DeWitt, April 2017a).

But, what is really innovative is doing what needs to be done to help shape the next education model—one where the academic and social-emotional success of all students is the only priority. Differentiating instruction for our students' needs is one of the ways to do this, and as indicated above, differentiated instruction is more effective when we consider the environment in which we try to implement it and adjust accordingly.

But how?

I wish I had a linear plan for how to systemically change our educational model. But I don't. I also recognize there are people who consider school reformers to be idealistic. I don't know, maybe we are.

I know there are steps educators can take to collectively propel us forward. Likewise, there are things we can do (or not do) to ensure we stay stagnant. It is up to us to decide which route we want to take. Country music singer Jimmy Dean was quoted in *Readers' Digest* saying, "I can't change the direction of the wind, but I can adjust my sails to always reach my destination" (Dean, 1987). I can't help but think that, maybe, if we all adjust our sails, we may actually have a shot at changing the direction of the wind.

Meet the Needs of All Students

We start by valuing the creativity and individuality of students by bringing their voice into *their* learning. We recognize the end goal is that all students participate in the symphony, playing different instruments at different levels of mastery to ultimately make beautiful music together.

We stop comparing students to each other. We compare them to themselves. How have they grown? Where do they need to go? We create environments where students naturally look at their peers and strive to improve because they see the results. When the learning environment is differentiated appropriately, intrinsic motivation is the result. Two questions become a thing of the past: When is this due? And, how much is this worth?

We recognize that learning does not know time and place. We recognize that learning happens in a variety of ways and accept and embrace this as a gift.

And, we stop judging content. Math is not more important than reading. Reading is not more important than art. Classic literature is not more important than young adult fiction. American History is not more important than Ancient History. It's the learning that is important. We use content to ensure our students can see the value in learning by exposing them to a variety of content, not making them experts in the topics we teachers happen to find most interesting. This all starts by reimagining our learning environments from the ground up. We cannot wait for systemic shifts to change. The system will shift when we force it to do so.

In his 2006 TED Talk, *Do Schools Kill Creativity?*, Sir Ken Robinson, eloquently makes a compelling plea to educators:

> Intelligence is wonderfully interactive. The brain isn't divided into compartments. In fact, creativity—which I define as the process of having original ideas that have value—more often than not comes about through the interaction of different disciplinary ways of seeing things . . . .

> All kids have tremendous talents. And we squander them, pretty ruthlessly. So I want to talk about education and I want to talk about creativity. My contention is that creativity now is as important in education as literacy . . . .

> What TED celebrates is the gift of the human imagination. We have to be careful now that we use this gift wisely and that we avert some of the scenarios that we've talked about. And the only way we'll do it is by seeing our creative capacities for the richness they are and seeing our children for the hope that they are. And our task is to educate their whole being, so they can face this future.

Keywords here are *interactive, creativity, talent, imagination, capacity, educate,* and *future*.

These are keywords for our students, but even more importantly for us, their teachers. How do we change the learning environment? We collaborate and use our talent, creativity, and imagination to design learning environments where we educate and build capacity in our students and each other for the future. We conduct symphonies, not fashion assembly lines for our students.

I first thought of the analogy on teaching and conducting an orchestra during the summer of 2015 as I embarked on my new role as a differentiation instructional coach. I was driving with my brother-in-law, Dean Westman, who is a world-renowned music educator. As I was telling him about my new job and anticipating some of the hallmarks of the need for differentiation (different ability levels, different interests, yet ultimately the same goal) I stopped myself and said to Dean, "This is what you and other music directors do on a daily basis. Differentiation is at the heart of your practice. How can we make this the model for education? Why have I never learned from a music, art, or PE teacher during PD time?"

From there, I would frequently chat with Dean and other band and orchestra directors to tap into the knowledge they possessed. Dean continued to be an inspiration for me due in large part to his outlook on education.

Teacher Voice

Dean Westman, Founder and Director of Orchestras, Performing Arts Department Chair

Bluecoats Program Coordinator

Avon High School

Avon, IN

As I enter my 24th year in education, I find myself thinking a lot about the simple principles that Maestro Livingston instilled in me as a young educator, and how those principles continue to resonate today. As music educators and in our case orchestra conductors, we come to work each day with a firm belief that every child needs to feel valued as an individual, a unique human being with endless potential. We also come to work each day understanding that those same students need to feel part of something bigger. They thrive off the idea of being part of a team, club, or in our case, orchestra. We use music as a vehicle to celebrate the individuals that makeup the orchestra (or band or choir), while relentlessly pursuing the group goal of making music at the highest level possible.

Granted, students who commit to the performing arts are generally pretty wonderful kids. At Avon High School, our award-winning symphony orchestra consists of students who will go on to study engineering, law, medicine, science, music, and every major in between. Is it sunshine and lollipops every day? Nope! The same challenges that a classroom teacher faces in a seventh-grade mathematics class are likely happening down the hallway in an eighth-grade band class . . . for that band director and all 80 students who are in the class. In a rehearsal, the most important thing is the conductor on the podium. The balance of information and inspiration that the conductor brings to each rehearsal defines the educational experience for those students. I venture to guess this is no different in a biology lab or English classroom.

One of the exciting challenges when conducting a musical ensemble is getting students to buy into the fact that music has no benchwarmers. I have 42 violinists in my symphony orchestra, and the range of talent within those 42 is mind blowing. It's not unusual for an administrator to walk into a rehearsal early in the semester, listen to what must sound like scratching and clawing, and then quickly exit the room. The sight-reading and learning of a major orchestral work is daunting.

(Continued)

(Continued)

The weeks that follow that initial "fright-read" of the music to the final performance of the piece can only be described as exhilarating. It's an experience that can feel chaotic, even when flawlessly planned out. It's a collaborative experience between the musicians and conductor. The process to get Violin 42 to play on the level of Violin 1 takes patience, understanding, love (sometimes tough love), and daily nurturing and guidance. I have never heard two musicians who sound the same. They might be of similar playing abilities, but every musician has a unique sound, technique, and expressive quality to their playing.

What a mathematics teacher may refer to as differentiated instruction or formative assessment, I simply call rehearsing. An English teacher may give a test at the end of a unit, or grading period to see if the students mastered the material. In my world, that is a concert. And although my subject may not have a standardized test, I will tell you that performing a famous Beethoven symphony in front of a packed concert hall is a very intimidating and very public way to assess whether or not your students have mastered the learning intentions.

We are all here to serve kids. Whether it is through music, science, physical education, social studies, language arts, mathematics, or a foreign language. We share the common goal of teaching our subject matter in a way that elevates the mind and inspires the soul. Every classroom is a symphony orchestra, full of unique human beings all wanting to be part of something special. Channel your inner Maestro to create the very best level of performance for all of your students!

Design Classrooms Conducive to Student-Driven Differentiation

Habituation: noun: reduction of psychological or behavioral response occurring when a specific stimulus occurs repeatedly (www.dictionary.com).

So, how can we emulate what Dean does with his orchestra in our classrooms? We can start with room arrangements. And, while we are discussing my family, let me tell you about another family member, my mother-in-law, Debbie Westman.

They say that men marry their mothers. And, while I certainly see many similarities between my mother-in-law and me, there is one stark difference. My mother-in-law is a skilled interior decorator who has done wonders arranging and rearranging my house. In contrast, I am a victim of **habituation**. I become so comfortable in my surroundings I never think to change them. As teachers, are we regularly changing and designing our learning environments, or are we creatures of habituation?

Recently, there has been a push to redesign classrooms with colorful and portable furniture and apparatuses. While this can certainly make things look pretty and perhaps more functional, we already have everything we need to create learning environments conducive for student-driven differentiation right at our fingertips. When I started playing around with classroom structure, I found the changes outlined in Figure 7.1 to be helpful.

Create an Environment for Positive Student Interaction

One of the criteria for creating a learning environment where learning is visible is by using the power of peer interaction to positively progress student learning (Hattie, 2012, p. 87).

Creating an environment where students can interact positively is directly related to building quality relationships and a strong rapport that is modeled by the teacher (see Chapter 1). Furthermore, student interaction (whether in small groups engaged in collaborative learning or partners) thrives on clear and realistic expectations.

Make Student Ownership Part of the Classroom Culture

There are a variety of ways learners can take control of their academic and social-emotional responsibilities. Sometimes, differentiating for students in this area is as simple as giving them options rather than mandating certain procedures. For instance, instead of mandating students write their homework

Figure 7.1   Suggestions for Rearranging Your Classroom

- Instead of having bookshelves and tables line the perimeter of the room, move them to divide the room into sections.
- Have students work in groups based on the skill(s) they are working to master, regardless of the content.
- Ask students to arrange and rearrange furniture on a daily basis. Create systems so that students do this efficiently.
- Ask students to work in small groups to design an ideal workspace.
- Ask students to decorate the room.
- Turn an empty closet into a recording studio or other workspace for specific projects.
- Allow students to work in ways that work best for them, which includes letting them listen to music if they choose. To avoid "finding a song," have students create playlists and save them in Google Drive.

assignments in an assignment notebook, encourage them to use tools or systems that work best for them to achieve the learning intention, in this case, keeping track of assignments. The key to learner responsibility is to give them a clear goal or objective and a few options on how to reach the objective. One of the options should always allow for students to come up with their own idea.

One of the best examples I have seen of student ownership of learning was in an eighth-grade physical education class taught by Jeff Priban at McCracken Middle School. Using data from their Fitnessgram tests, Jeff asked students to set goals for themselves in the areas of flexibility, endurance, and strength. He then collaborated with them to create action plans while simultaneously providing instruction around how these three areas work together. Jeff conferred with each student to determine how much time and what type of activities should be completed in each area, and what success in each of these areas would look like. Students then monitored their progress toward their goals on a daily basis (**formative assessment**) to eventually be assessed again by the Fitnessgram (**summative assessment**).

A visitor to Jeff's class in the fitness center would see students engaged in a variety of tasks all chosen by them, according to their assessment of what they need to do to accomplish their individual fitness goals. Some students would be using iPads to participate in a yoga class on their flexibility goals, some students would use the cardio machines to work toward their endurance goals, and others would be using weights or bands or doing calisthenics to meet their strength goals. Mr. Priban walks around with a clipboard formatively assessing students and giving them feedback throughout the class, which ranges from task related (you did 20 sit-ups) to feedback that promotes self-regulation (can you tell me why you have chosen to work on flexibility 3 days this week?).

The premise that Jeff uses in his classroom can work in any content area and grade level, again with the right tools and instructional strategies. And, perhaps the best options for teachers to use to encourage learner responsibility, set, and monitor progress toward goals is by using digital portfolios.

Learner Responsibility Through Digital Portfolios

In the age of blended classrooms and digital learning, the popularity of student portfolios has exponentially increased. Digital student portfolios can continue to be used for their original purpose of highlighting work that the teacher or student is particularly proud of. Parents will no longer have to take up closet space or secretly dispose of paper portfolios when their children go to sleep (no judgment, parents—I get it).

Using student portfolios as a tool to help increase student learning in addition to showcasing final projects is a relatively new take on an old tradition. There are ways to use digital portfolios that align with some of the instructional practices with the highest effect size as found by Hattie's research, such as:

1. *Student Goal Setting (.5).* Back to the basics. Ask your students to set goals by using data. For each of the three *Rs*—reading, writing, and arithmetic—have students determine three skills-based or standard-aligned goals. Goals should be skills-based to make them applicable to as many content areas as possible. Students can then document their rise toward meeting their goals in all of their classes by adding examples of work that show growth.

2. *Teacher Student Feedback (.75).* As you assess your students' work, add items to their portfolios with actionable feedback. For example, you have a student who struggled with a portion of an assignment. You can highlight this assignment and add the item to the student's portfolio with your feedback, "You seem to be struggling with comprehending this text. What other strategy could you try?" When the student tries another strategy and succeeds, you add the new item with new feedback, "Performing a focused read really seemed to help you comprehend this text. What do you think was the difference?"

3. *Student tracking progress toward mastery (1.44).* Have students assess their own work using a rubric that you have co-created with them. They can do this digitally, on paper and upload, create and upload a video, or use a variety of other mediums to add their self-assessment to their portfolios.

4. *Examples of mastery learning (.58).* When students are able to see examples of work at different levels (approaching, meets, exceeds standards, or A, B, C, D), they are able to better understand what is expected of them. Use this year's student portfolios to help inform next year's students of expectations.

5. *School–home communication (.52).* Student portfolios can promote the school–home relationship as they provide more than just a grade. Student portfolios become the vehicle for driving parent–teacher conferences and furthermore encourage constant and consistent conversation between parents, teachers, and students. I used the Otus Student Performance Platform to have students build their portfolios complete with examples of my feedback and their responses to show their growth in real time. In Otus, students

and teachers can exchange feedback directly in documents and in rubrics that are side-by-side with assessments. Visit https://otus.com to find out more.

Poetry Focused Reading

Directions: Read the poem below and identify where the author uses an adjective to describe a noun.

*I want someone who make me change the way I feel today
'Cause now I feel like someone who
Is overdue for someone like you*

*I want a love that I can't hide
I want the simple things in life*

*I've always had a simple way with words
But when I'm with you I get so confused
Can't you see just what I want to say?
I'm in love, I'm in love!*

Poetry Focused Reading

Directions: Read the poem below and identify where the author uses an adjective to describe a noun.

*I want someone who make me change the way I feel today
'Cause now I feel like someone who
Is overdue for someone like you*

*I want a love that I can't hide
I want the simple things in life*

*I've always had a simple way with words
But when I'm with you I get so confused
Can't you see just what I want to say?
I'm in love, I'm in love!*

This list is by no means a comprehensive compilation of ways you can use student portfolios. As with everything in this book, these are provisional examples that can be tweaked to best work in your classroom. And, student portfolios are just one way to promote learner responsibility. Figure 7.2 offers some additional ways to accomplish promoting learner responsibility.

Figure 7.2   Additional Suggestions for Promoting Learner
Responsibility

- Model *a variety* of ways students can record their outstanding assignments such as on a paper calendar, digital calendar with or without alerts, sending themselves an email with a time delay (the Chrome store offers a variety of free extensions that can do this).

- Allow students to *build their own library* of resources using a learning management system (if you are 1:1) *or* using empty crates or boxes for print materials.

- Frequently ask students to reflect to *determine which strategies work best for them and why.*

Guide Students in Setting Their Own Goals

What is the best way to promote student ownership? Engage in *goal setting*.

As I mentioned in Chapter 6, once I saw the impact goal setting had on student growth, I was sold. As an instructional coach, I worked closely with many teachers to help them gain a better understanding of goal setting and how they would benefit from taking class time to goal set with students. Samantha Mason reflects on this process in the following vignette. She describes four steps to quality goal setting in regard to an adaptive test her students were taking. The same principles can be applied to all goal setting.

Teacher Voice

Samantha Mason, Sixth-Grade English Language Arts Teacher

Formerly of Skokie School District 73.5

Skokie, IL

Four Steps to Quality Goal Setting

1. **Goals must be feasible.** The first step to creating a solid action plan is to make sure the plan is realistic. Setting realistic goals is difficult, especially when you are excited and determined to do your absolute best. Our instructional coach shared a story about her husband's desire to lose weight. His initial plan was to go on a diet and lose 30

(Continued)

(Continued)

pounds the first month. I could see the eyes of my students widen as they realized this plan was not possible, or healthy. The same realistic mindset should be taken into consideration when setting Measure of Academic Progress (MAP) goals (Northwest Evaluation Association, 2013). Students were asked to think about the amount of time between now and the next testing period when creating their action plans.

2. **Goals and action plans must be measurable.** Measurable action plans enable students to stay on track to meet their goals. They also must be clear and include direct evidence. It is important to think about how the student is going to monitor their progress. Each child already had a measurable goal in place, their MAP goal, but the steps within the action plan needed to be visible as well. The coach continued the story about her husband and asked the students how he would know if he was successful. They quickly replied, "A scale!" This example was extremely helpful during individual conferences with students. If a student suggested their action plan would include reading more each night, we directed them to attach a specific time limit or number of pages that made sense for their lifestyle.

3. **Goals must be sustainable.** During many of the conversations I observed, students claimed they would work toward their goal on a daily basis. While this might be the case for a select few, most are going to be dedicating a few days each week to their action plan. Our coach reminded students their action plan must be maintainable, and they should think about other events that occur during the week. We asked students to bring their assignment notebooks during our goal-setting conversations to pencil in specific times during the week.

4. **Goals must be meaningful.** Most importantly, the action plan must be meaningful to each individual. If they are important and motivating, there is a greater chance of achievement. I was amazed by some of the action plans students were creating such as completing vocabulary activities on the app Elevate or creating word-search games using unfamiliar words. The options were endless.

Use Technology to Promote Learning and Creativity

When people refer to 21st century learning, the first thing that often comes to mind is technology. The use of technology in and of itself will not change instruction. In fact, depending on how technology is used, it can either powerfully impact or critically hinder student-driven differentiation.

Teaching is hard work. It is rewarding, but let's be real, it is also physically, emotionally, and mentally exhausting. Because teaching is so exhausting, it can be tempting to look for shortcuts and silver bullets to make instruction easier. In *Stratosphere*: author Michael Fullan summarizes this (2013), "the scariest part about the new technologies is that they give people the false sense that they are learning something new just by using an elegant machine" (p. 60).

I often see this with the use of online worksheets or multiple-choice quizzes. There are countless options for using digital tools to quiz students, and many of these offer "built-in differentiation" in the form of leveled worksheets or readings. Some of these options are initially super exciting, and students love them. But once the novelty wears off, students are once again just do the same old thing, and even though the worksheets or readings maybe differentiated at their level, their voice has not been considered at all.

Student-driven differentiation thrives with the appropriate use of technology. There is certainly a time and place for digital learning resources, but like everything, in moderation. More importantly, student-driven differentiation calls for technology to be used to allow learning to be as relevant as possible for students and allow them to engage and create.

While I am a proponent of designing learning opportunities and culminating activities that naturally lend themselves to student interest, ownership, and result in achievement, there are times when teachers and students need breaks from designing elaborate projects and give students times to do their own thing. The right technology can do this for students.

How to Ensure Technology Positively Impacts Differentiation

Focus on Producing Not Consuming

Dr. Ruben Puentedura coined the acronym SAMR (substitution, augmentation, modification, redefinition) in 2013 which gives educators a taxonomy (similar to Bloom's taxonomy or Webb's Depth of Knowledge) that teachers can use to determine the level at which they are using technology.

Bloom's taxonomy: categorization of levels of human learning

Webb's Depth of Knowledge (DoK): classifies tasks according to the complexity of thinking required to successfully complete them

When practicing student-driven differentiation, there is a place for all levels of SAMR from time to time, but I would caution teachers to ask themselves if they are making the learning experience as relevant as possible if they are not at the level of M (modification) or R (redefinition). Take a look at the example outlined in Figure 7.3

Figure 7.3 The SAMR Model

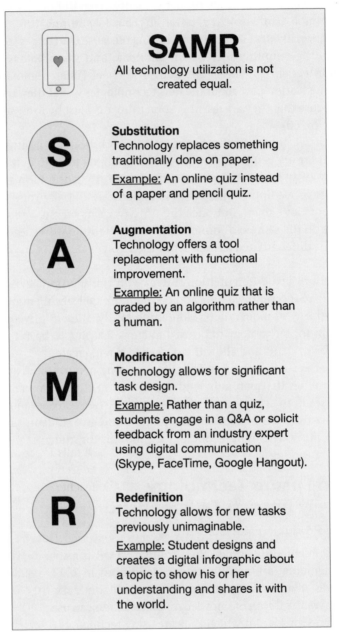

The S (substitution) and A (augmentation) certainly have a place in learning and assessing, but looking at the M (modification) and R (redefinition), we see how learning shifts from consuming and regurgitating to producing. When looking at the SAMR model within the context of differentiating the learning environment, the focus is on creating conditions to encourage the four *C*s of learning: communication, collaboration, creativity, and critical thinking. Refer to Chapter 6 for examples of technology-infused projects that allowed for creation rather than just consumption.

Choose Technology Tools and Online Curricula Wisely

"Learners are the driver and technology is the accelerator." (Couros, 2015, p. 148)

There is absolutely a time and place for the use for technology, and the way I see it is there are three types of EdTech tools:

1. Tools that allow for student and teacher innovation (examples: movie-making tools, blogging tools, infographic makers, Google Apps for Education)

2. Tools that can make learning more efficient for the student and teaching more efficient for the teacher (student performance platforms, learning management systems, Google, YouTube)

3. Tools that make assessing more efficient (automatic grading programs)

If a tool or curriculum falls into Categories 1 or 2, the technology addition is likely advantageous. However, if the tool falls into Category 3, I caution all educators to ask themselves: "Are your EdTech tools innovating student learning, or are they trying to replace the teacher?" Specifically, is there a tool that you are using to make your job easier but adds little or no value for students?

I think back to my impetus for starting to use Google Docs in my classroom. My students and I had a mutual need; we wanted to be able to collaborate on the same document, we wanted to be better able to manage drafts of papers, we wanted to avoid printing issues. We found a tech solution that met that need in Google Docs. Google Docs enabled more effective and efficient collaboration methods and feedback capabilities; however, Google Docs still allowed me to gain insight into who my students were as people and what their passions are. Knowing this information was vital for me to direct students to further their passions. See Chapter 8 for examples of how student choice can engage students in meaningful ways to deepen their own learning.

Teachers and students will always have needs and will always look for solutions. Once I saw a tweet from an educator who asked for recommendations for the "best app or program to grade essays and short answer questions." Many people responded with suggestions, but it seemed that even more offered words of caution about using a tech tool for a skill that really requires the human brain: *Sentence length can cause erroneous score; grammar errors that are actually correct are highlighted as being wrong; no ability to understand student voice or inflection.* Regardless of the disclaimers, apps that have been created to grade student writing may make teaching more efficient, but they certainly do not promote innovation or help foster a growth mindset in our students. In fact, due to the lack of appropriate feedback and removal of the human relationship piece that is vital to learning, I believe tools like this may be detrimental to student growth.

I do realize the problem automated grading systems solve: *having to physically grade.* In the traditional sense of the word, grading takes a lot of time . . . *for the teacher. Writing* can also take a lot of time . . . *for the student.* Time is an extremely valuable commodity, but so is learning. If a tech tool only makes grading more efficient, it really isn't an innovation **tool** at all— it's simply a way to remove the teacher from the assessment process. Of course, there are times when this can be helpful (i.e., multiple-choice items, true-or-false questions, etc.). But when students are being asked to share their thinking through writing, a computer algorithm just can't do what a teacher can do with regard to critical feedback or feedback beyond spelling and grammar check.

This may not be a popular notion, but it's true. Some tools may solve a problem only for teachers, which is totally fine. But some of these tools do so at the expense of student learning.

> Some tools may solve a problem only for teachers, which is totally fine. But some of these tools do so at the expense of student learning.

For years, I struggled to find a "packaged" curriculum (web based or not) that would allow students to work individually or in small groups on appropriately tiered curriculum aligned to their interests and strengths. Then I was introduced to the web-based product, Thrively, and jackpot! Thrively did all of this, while building students' self-esteem and allowing them to connect with students around the world with similar interests.

So, in June of 2016, when I met Thrively's Founder, Girish Venkat, at ISTE, I was not surprised to hear that Girish's impetus for creating Thrively was student voice. The student was his son. In the following reflection, Girish tells the story of creating a web-based learning program that gives all students an opportunity to pursue their passion.

Parent Voice

Girish Venkat, Creator and Founder

Thrively

Glendale, CA

Thrively started as a personal journey for me as a dad watching my son Rohit grow up. Rohit was doing fine academically, but like most of the kids his age, he was glued to TV and video games. I didn't see the passion in him nor was he driven. He was struggling to find purpose in his life. I was pushing him to learn coding, to build stuff (mostly computers and electronics related, as I happen to be an electronics and communication engineer). He wasn't interested. I knew this was an age where kids' first reaction is a no when you ask them to do something, and that is especially true if it comes from the parents, so I kept at it. But I realized after a couple of years what a lame parent I was being! I call this my "lame parent" moment. It was clear to me that I was pushing my son to do what I wanted him to do rather than trying to understand what he wanted to do. I started asking myself:

1. *How do I help my son discover what he is good at and what his strengths are?* Parents and schools always point out what kids are not good at and what they should be good at, but don't celebrate what they actually are good at. The result is that a kid's self-esteem and enthusiasm take a beating at an early age, and they become disengaged.

2. *How do I expose my son to all the opportunities for enrichment out there?* As kids get more exposure, they will eventually find their passion. Some kids find this early, and for some, it takes several years.

3. *How do I help my son explore his interests and aspirations?*

This was just the seed of an idea, but the vision for Thrively started taking shape in my mind then.

As I was struggling with the questions above and how I was going to help my son find his passion, a few things happened. I read *Outliers* (2013) by Malcolm Gladwell, I met some key people like Jennifer Fox, author of *Your Child's Strengths* (2008)*,* and started meeting with pediatric neuropsychologists. *Your Child's Strengths* triggered a lot of ideas about how I should approach building Thrively.

From my meetings with Jennifer Fox and pediatric neuropsychologists, I learned that every human is born with the same number of brain cells. As the brain gets stimulated, the connection between the brain cells increases, thereby increasing how much information the brain can process.

(Continued)

(Continued)

We kid ourselves that people are born with the greatness gene. All kids can learn, but not in the same way or at the same time. Every child is different and special, but we put them all in a class and teach everyone the same subject in the same way and expect each of them to magically develop as individuals.

All of this got me thinking about how different the world would be if parents and educators were equipped with all this information and could expose the kids to all the enrichment customized to their children's strengths. Thrively was founded on a core philosophy that every child has a genius, and they deserve to thrive (hence the name *thrive-ly*).

To me, this was clearly the next disruption needed in the education space: personalized strength-based education. Personalized learning is not about kids learning at their own pace (how most schools see personalizing learning), but about self-directed learning by kids based on their strengths and what they are passionate about. That is true personalized learning! We at Thrively are at the forefront of driving this disruption.

I am happy to say that through Thrively, Rohit found his passion and is now a sophomore pursuing his interests in game design and computer science at the Rochester Institute of Technology (RIT). As for Thrively, I am delighted to be able to say we are collaborating with tens of thousands of educators and parents to uncover every kid's strengths and help them find their passion in life so they can thrive.

Monitor Student Progress Toward Learning Intentions

One of the questions I get asked most frequently is, how do you monitor student progress if each student is potentially at a different place in his or her learning? My answer to this is always, know what your learning intentions and success criteria are, and if possible, use web-based tools, as this is a prime example of when technology can make learning more efficient. Using digital proficiency scales or rubrics like some of the examples illustrated earlier in the chapter can be helpful for you and students to know when mastery has been met.

> Record keeping should be done by learning intention or standard, not completion of assignments.

Then, use a record keeping system that works for you. Record keeping should be done by learning intention or standard, not completion of assignments.

When students show mastery of the learning intentions and success criteria as you have prescribed, you can collaborate with them to determine where they go next in their learning, while the rest of their classmates are still progressing toward mastery. The key is to remember that you are using formative assessment to determine when mastery has been achieved, and that means students will not all have the same number of formative assessments to show mastery; some may show mastery after three and some may need ten assessments.

Figures 7.4 and 7.5 are examples of what record keeping can look like using a web-based student performance platform or a standard spreadsheet (student names are fictional):

Enlist Parents' Help in Furthering Student Learning

As stated at the beginning of this chapter, traditional school systems (aka the factory model of teaching) have been in place since the early twentieth century. This means all parents and grandparents of students currently in kindergarten through twelfth grade, plus the vast majority of today's teachers experienced school with the factory model of instruction. A shift in education can feel threatening to parents because we are removing a critical piece of their identity formation.

Figure 7.4   Monitoring the Mastery of Learning Intentions Online

GRADING PERIOD	Identify Claim	Identify Claim	Identify Claim	Support Evidence	Support Evidence	Support Evidence	Support Evidence
SELECT / DESELECT ALL	☑	☑	☑	☑	☐	☐	☐
Patrick Quinn	☑	☑	☑	☑	☑	☐	☐
Carrie Fitzgerald	☑	☑	☑	☑	☑	☐	☐
Nora Nguyen	☑	☑	☑	☑	☐	☐	☐
Matthew Hubbard	☑	☑	☑	☑	☐	☐	☐
Eugene Little	☑	☑	☑	☑	☑	☐	☐
Gary Long	☑	☑	☑	☑	☐	☐	☑
Alta Carroll	☑	☑	☑	☑	☐	☐	☑
Maria Stevenson	☑	☑	☑	☑	☐	☑	☐
Brent Bradley	☑	☑	☑	☑	☐	☑	☑
Gavin Barnes	☑	☑	☑	☑	☐	☑	☐
Donald Moran	☑	☑	☑	☑	☐	☐	☐
Michael Gold	☑	☑	☑	☑	☐	☑	☐

Source: Example from Otus Student Performance System. www.otus.com

Figure 7.5   Monitoring the Mastery of Learning Intentions on a Spreadsheet

Unit: Short Stories	Compare and contrast two or more characters, settings, or events in a story or drama, drawing on specific details in the text (e.g., how characters interact).				Key E—exceeds M—mastered A—approaching N—not yet N/A—not assessed P—pre-assessment F—formative S—summative *E indicates student is working on material not assessed in the curriculum to extend learning.
Dates →	2/1	2/2	2/3	2/4	2/5
Keller	N	A	A	M	Ex
Mallory	E	N/A	N/A	N/A	N/A
Scott	M	N/A	M	N/A	N/A
Sloane	A	A	N/A	M	M
Will	N	N	A	N/A	M
Abby	A	A	M	M	E
Paige	M	M	N/A	E	N/A
Jack	A	M	M	A	M
Brielle	N	M	N/A	M	M
Halie	N	N	N	N	A

It can be hard for teachers to navigate conversations about shifts in education with parents. It is critical that teachers communicate clearly (see Chapter 1 for tips on communicating). Remaining composed can be difficult when facing an angry parent who is questioning your practices (such as differentiation). Nevertheless, it is essential that you remain calm and clearly and appropriately explain how every child's needs will be met in this new system. I hope you find some useful tips in Figure 7.6.

Figure 7.6   Parent Communication Hacks

Parent Communication Hacks

That Will Change Your Practice!

Do Not	Do

Give attribute praise. *"Your child is smart."*

Give specific examples. *"Your child takes initiative with problem solving, for example . . ."*

Blame the child. *"I have explained to your child why it is important to pay attention and he continues to choose to be disengaged."*

Consider your role. *"I am working to incorporate ways to better engage your son in the learning process. I will keep you updated on our progress."*

Assume status. *"Your child's behavior is not appropriate for 'x' grade and he knows that. Please reinforce these behavior expectations at home."*

Presuppose the parent is your partner. *"I wanted to discuss how I have been addressing some issues in the classroom to see if you find similar success at home."*

Use educational jargon. *"Your child has qualified for a Tier 2 intervention for reading."*

Provide a concise explanation. *"Recent assessment results show your child will benefit from a reading comprehension intervention."*

Discussion Questions

▶ How can music education be a model for our changing classrooms?

▶ How can you redesign your learning environment to be more conducive to your students' needs?

▶ What are some ways you can monitor and record the progress of your students so you can flexibly group and pace? How can digital portfolios help?

▶ What role does goal setting play in student ownership?

▶ What questions should you ask yourself before choosing technology tools or online curricula?

Visit the companion website at http://resources.corwin .com/studentdrivendifferentiation.

Chapter 8

The Role of Choice in Meeting Learning Intentions

While reading *The Paradox of Choice: Why More Is Less* (2016) by Barry Schwartz, I was fascinated by the effect choice has on the human psyche. My learning from this book changed my approach to simple tasks like grocery shopping and more complex matters like child-rearing and teaching. Schwartz writes:

> When people have no choice, life is almost unbearable. As the number of available choices increases, as it has in our consumer culture, the autonomy, control, and liberation this variety brings are powerful and positive. But as the number of choices keeps growing, negative aspects of having a multitude of options begin to appear. As the number of choices grows further, the negatives escalate until we become overloaded. At this point, choice no longer liberates, but debilitates. (p. 2)

Schwartz suggests that being faced with too many options causes many people to choose nothing, which ultimately leads to disappointment. Here we see a paradox: Having choice is vital, but too many options to choose from is destructive (Schwartz, 2016, pp. 2–3).

This holds true for both teachers and students and is one of the reasons I chose to limit the number of examples and strategies I outline in this book. We need to do the same thing for students: We need to offer them appropriate choices that allow them to exert their autonomy and build their efficacy. Those choices also need to be appropriately aligned to the learning intentions. Choices shouldn't be so numerous that they overwhelm the student.

Offer Choices That Fulfill Learning Needs

It is important to note that offering students choice alone does not necessarily meet their needs, nor does it allow them ownership of their learning.

> Offering students choice alone does not necessarily meet their needs, nor does it allow them ownership of their learning.

For instance, I frequently give my children a choice of what they want to eat for dinner. One time, I let them choose between McDonald's, Burger King, or Wendy's. While they may have voted me "mom of the year," I certainly didn't offer them the best choices for their nutritional needs. As teachers, we sometimes offer students choices that are not appropriate for their needs and may even muddy the learning process when the learning intentions are not clear.

Take, for example, the tic-tac-toe style choice board that many teachers give students. Students get to "choose" learning activities based on their personal preference, not necessarily their need. For teachers, this may seem like differentiating, but without a targeted goal, action plan, or progression, students are just working to complete different tasks, not necessarily growing.

Take a look at the example of a choice board on the US Constitution, shown in Figure 8.1.

While some of the tasks on this choice board may meet the needs of certain students, the likelihood that students will choose the three in a row (assuming the boxes are aligned) they need to grow academically, is improbable. Additionally, the idea that a student would be able to clearly understand the learning intentions and success criteria from this choice board is highly improbable. Instead, offer students choice (in choice boards or other formats) by using student learning progressions and options that allow them to once again have control over some of the content. In contrast to the tic-tac-toe board in Figure 8.1, look at the stair-step example

Figure 8.1   Constitution Tic-Tac-Toe

Pick three tasks to win across, up/down, or diagonally.

Create a list of all of the amendments and include a summary.	Write a song that would be a good slogan for one of our current candidate's campaign.	Write a paragraph summarizing the Bill of Rights.
Draw a poster illustrating your favorite part of our Constitution unit.	Create a T-chart of the pros and cons of the two-term limit for president.	Make a timeline of the events leading up to the first Constitutional Convention.
Write two paragraphs answering this question: Which amendment is in the most need of modification and why?	Explain what the three branches of government do.	Write a journal entry pretending you are a candidate running for president. Talk about your campaign.

in Figure 8.2, which includes a civics learning progression from the social studies C3 Framework.

By considering student need in addition to student choice, teachers can more effectively differentiate to ensure students' needs are met resulting in academic and social-emotional growth.

Incorporating student voice comes next. To include student voice appropriately focus on the following questions:

▶ What is the learning intention for this lesson or unit?

▶ What prior knowledge do students need to complete this?

▶ How will I incorporate student voice to find relevant applications of this concept or skill?

▶ How can my students provide input on what the success criteria could look like and create options for demonstrating learning?

▶ How will I provide feedback?

Figure 8.2   Stair-Step Choice Approach to Differentiating Learning Intentions

D2.Civ.1.9–12:
Distinguish the powers and responsibilities of local, state, tribal, national, and international civic and political institutions.

C3.Civics Standard:D2.Civ.6–8: *Distinguish the powers and responsibilities of citizens (such as voters, jurors, taxpayers, members of the armed forces, petitioners, protesters, and office-holders).*

D2.Civ.3–5: *Distinguish the responsibilities and powers of government officials at various levels and branches of government and in different times and places.*

Learning Intention

I can *explain* how power and responsibilities of citizens were different during different eras of history.

Learning Intention

I can *compare/contrast* two groups of citizens, their powers, and their responsibilities.

Learning Intention

I can *describe* the powers of citizens.

Learning Intention

I can *describe* the responsibilities of citizens.

Task Choice	**Task Choice**	**Task Choice**	**Task Choice**
Click here for examples of the success criteria	*Click here for examples of the success criteria*	*Click here for examples of the success criteria*	*Click here for examples of the success criteria*
Write 2–3 paragraphs detailing research *~OR~* Create a visual to represent research	Write 2–3 paragraphs detailing research *~OR~* Create a visual to represent research	Create a Venn diagram or other visual *~OR~* Create two logical superheroes that represent each group and explain their powers/responsibilities	Research a period of history and write an essay *~OR~* Research a period of history and 'interview' someone (real or fictional) from the time *~OR~*

Example 1: Use Choice as Part of Curriculum Compacting

What do you get when you add these variables together?

▶ Pre-assessment data

▶ Student goal setting

▶ Rigorous curriculum

▶ Student interest

▶ Student choice

▶ Expanding the walls of the typical classroom

▶ Authentic resources

▶ Authentic audience

▶ Authentic products

Well, one answer is passion projects. According to Cash (2010), passion projects

▶ Are inquiry based

▶ Rely on concepts, rather than just facts

▶ Involve critical reasoning

▶ Encourage creative thinking

▶ Require problem-solving (and problem-finding)

▶ Encourage reflection

▶ Use the assessment for learning cycle (p. 63)

Several years ago, my English Language Arts (ELA) colleagues and I offered passion projects to students who qualified for an extension (through curriculum compacting). We found this extension opportunity to be highly engaging and appropriately challenging for students.

My colleagues and I collaborated with students to design interest-based, need-targeted, individual projects that allowed students to collaborate on the process. We started with a pre-assessment on a unit of the features of nonfiction versus fiction, as outlined by our textbook series, to determine who needed curriculum compacting and then used information gathered from an adaptive assessment (Northwest Evaluation Association, 2013) to help students design their projects. As stated earlier in this chapter, it is rare just to differentiate one area (content, process, product, learning environment), and likely all areas are affected. See the passion project examples in Figures 8.3 and 8.4 as evidence of this.

Figure 8.3   Standards-Aligned Passion Projects

Standards	Interest-Based, Need-Targeted, Individual Projects
RL1:	Cite several pieces of textual evidence to support analysis of what the text says explicitly as well as inferences drawn from the text.
RL2:	Determine a theme or central idea of a text and analyze its development over the course of the text; provide an objective summary of the text.
RI2:	Determine two or more central ideas in a text and analyze their development over the course of the text; provide an objective summary of the text.
RI8:	Trace and evaluate the argument and specific claims in a text, assessing whether the reasoning is sound and the evidence relevant and sufficient to support the claims.

Figure 8.4   Louie's Passion Project

CONTENT: MAP GOAL AREA (circle one):

Literature   Vocabulary   Informational Text

PASSION: Debating Politics

PROCESS AS INFORMED BY STUDENT: Read **Animal Farm,** while simultaneously reading (class read) **Fahrenheit 451.** Compare fictional political systems in literature and the commentary they make on actual political systems.

PRODUCT AS DETERMINED BY STUDENT: After going through the process, it

was determined that Louie would use the knowledge from his process to engage in a Skype meeting with FOX News Legal Correspondent, Tamara Holder. Louie then was able to ask and discuss a series of questions related to the novels read as well as other political questions. Louie shared his experience with his classmates.

Image used with permission.

Figure 8.5   Jillian's Passion Project

CONTENT: MAP GOAL AREA (circle one):

Literature   Vocabulary   (Informational Text)

PASSION: Fashion

PROCESS AS INFORMED BY STUDENT: Research fashion and predict a fall fashion trend that will inform a critique of current fashion.

PRODUCT AS DETERMINED BY STUDENT: After going through the process, it was determined that Jillian would be a guest blogger on the popular fashion blog **Possessionista**. She worked with the founder of the blog, Dana Weiss (2014), to research, curate, and publish her guest blog.

PROJECT RUNWAY FASHION RECAP: A GUEST POST BY JILLIAN S., AGE 12

A few weeks ago I was introduced to 12-year old Jillian S. an aspiring fashion designer who's often found practicing her ice skating routines in her self-designed costumes. (How cool is that?) Jillian was assigned a project where she has to write and be published for an audience, and naturally I was so impressed by this well-spoken, and savvy young fashionista that I invited her to contribute to Possessionista with a weekly recap of her favorite show: Project Runway. I hope you'll all support Jillian in her efforts – she worked incredibly hard on this and tune in to **Facebook** *each week as Jillian recaps the hits and misses of Project Runway. (Thanks Jillian!)*

Dana Weiss, http://www.possessionista.com/

Example 2: Align Choice to Learning Intentions

I once had the serendipitous experience of working with two teams of fourth-grade teachers (from different districts) who were determining the success criteria for the Standard: CCSS.ELA-LITERACY.W.4.2: Write informative/explanatory texts to examine a topic and convey ideas and information clearly.

Each team had very different approaches to determining the success criteria for this standard. Team A insisted that all students wrote informative

Learning progressions represent prerequisite knowledge and skills that students must acquire incrementally before they are able to understand and apply more complex or advanced concepts and skills (Ainsworth & Viegut, 2015, p.178).

texts on the same topic, specifically owls, as they were studying owls in science. Team B decided to allow students to choose *any* content matter that they wanted. What was the result? Many students from both Team A and Team B struggled.

Students on Team A lacked autonomy in the learning process, and students on Team B struggled to pick topics because the range of options was so immense (paradox of choice).

Team B was quick to make changes and adapt the way they had students choose topics. Team A, however, struggled. They wanted to keep the topic of owls even though the standard they were assessing (write informative/explanatory texts to examine a topic and convey ideas and information clearly) had nothing to do with owls. When I asked them why, their response was, "Essays are easier for us to grade when all students have the same topic."

After further discussion and examination of the learning intentions (pulled directly from the language of the standard they were assessing), Team A agreed to try incorporating student voice and choice.

Interestingly, the ultimate result was same for both teams, they met somewhere in the middle and offered a reasonable number of topic choices. And, the list was created by the students to ensure the topics were relevant to *them*.

To facilitate creating this list, as the authentic hook for the unit, the teachers led students in a brief, whole-group discussion. Then the whole group broke into smaller groups, and students sorted the topics into three categories. Together, the teachers and students came to consensus and created a visual of the three categories and topics within each category. When students reached the point of choosing a topic, they could consult this list they had a part in making. The teachers all added asterisks for students who elected to write about something not on the list should they have another interest. Figure 8.6 demonstrates how the personalities of the class are collectively represented and allow students appropriate choice.

Example 3: Incorporate Choice in Homework Assignments

Over the past few years, I have had the opportunity to connect with educators who teach all subjects and grade levels, and I have seen many excellent examples of incorporating choice for homework should educators determine a need to assign it (it should be noted that research shows homework

Figure 8.6   Students Brainstorm Topic Choices

Team A

Current Events	Pop Culture	Places	Animals
• 2016 presidential election • Cubs win the World Series • Prince's death	• YouTube as a career • *Harry Potter* as a movie • *Harry Potter* as a book series • American Girl dolls	• the Amazon rainforest • Gettysburg, Virginia • the North Pole • the ocean	• owls • cats • dogs • snakes • leeches • endangered species *something else not on this list

Team B

People	Experiences	Technology
• our principal • the police department • emergency medical technicians (ambulance drivers) • Michael Jordan • R. J. Palacio • Steve Jobs	• sky diving • BMXing • skateboarding • cheerleading • bullying	• gaming • PC versus MAC • electric cars • hover boards • the Musically app • Snapchat *something else not on this list

has little to no effect on student growth in the elementary grades and a modest impact on students in middle and high school) (Hattie, 2012, p. 15).

High school Spanish teacher Zach Peterson, from Olentangy Local School District in Lewis Center, Ohio, sees student choice as a critical piece of learning a foreign language and sees homework as the vehicle to make homework personal for students increasing the likelihood that the student work done at home permeates learning *at* school as well.

Philosophically, Zach believes that students should "have the choice to fit the curriculum (in any content area) into their lives." Therefore, Zach does not assign homework, but creates compelling scenarios in something he calls "collab labs," which are authentic learning centers co-designed by the students and which entice them to continue their learning outside of class. When students choose to communicate outside of class, they use Voxer (a free app for smartphones and computers) because (1) Voxer is efficient and (2) Voxer allows students to communicate verbally and practice the most important skills in acquiring a foreign language: speaking.

Zach often says that students' (and adults') greatest fear is public speaking and when that public speaking is in a foreign language, the fear is exponentially increased. Voxer helps remove some of this fear as the live audience component is not a factor and students choose when and what they are going to communicate to their classmates.

Zach has found that allowing students to choose whether or not to work on Spanish class projects outside of class also transfers into speaking in the classroom. In Zach's room, students are not always in their "collab labs" but often learn in a more "traditional" approach: direct instruction and guided practice. During this time, Zach uses formative assessment information to **scaffold learning:** the practice of providing direct instruction and support for students as they acquire a skill or knowledge and gradually release the supports in place as they grow in their understanding (Wormeli & Tomlinson, 2007, p. 97).

Zach uses a simple formative assessment method to determine what scaffolds his students needs. He asks them one question, *"¿Podemos conversar en espanol?"* "Can we talk in Spanish?" If students answer they *can,* but they are afraid, he lets them demonstrate this in another way: Voxer, writing, etc. If students indicate that they can't yet communicate their question or answer in Spanish, Zach asks them to speak it in English. Zach uses this student feedback to help him form small groups for targeted instruction on either the skill/content or to practice speaking in a smaller group. As Zach has incorporated the choice of using Voxer to work on Spanish curriculum outside of class, he has seen his students' progress at faster rates and be more engaged in the process.

Example 4: Use Choice to Give Students Ownership of Their Own Learning

One of the most impressive and effective examples of giving students choice is when choice is built into the learning environment for students and students consistently have the same variety of choices every day. Middle school Math teacher Kirk Humphreys welcomes teachers from across the country into his classroom on a regular basis so they can see how he has embedded choice into his math curriculum and instruction.

Teacher Voice

Kirk Humphreys, Sixth- to Eighth-Grade Accelerated Math

Caruso Middle School

Deerfield, IL

After 10 years of giving math content by lecture, I made the change to the flipped classroom to make better use of class time. Students have access to my videos online to watch at home or in class. Class time is spent on collaborative activities and practice to reinforce concepts learned in the videos. The flipped classroom allows me to step aside while students take control of the class. I now have the entire class period to walk around and have conversations and give feedback to students. Over the last 5 years, my classroom has evolved to give students choice in all aspects of their learning in the following ways:

Learning Environment

Students take ownership not only of what they learn, but also as a class. At the beginning of class, a student volunteers to discuss the concepts learned in the current video. Students call on each other to continue the learning process. Students also answer questions from each other. I observe but do not intervene, even if a mistake is made. It is quite important for students not to rely on me to step in when mistakes are made. This entire process must be modeled at the beginning of the school year to show students what is expected.

Students have the entire class to collaborate and work on practice. This practice may be activities, practice problems, or student-created problems. Students have choice in what they are currently working on within my math classroom. I give an end date in which the standards for the unit must be met. Students are always given the standards before the unit begins. They know the expectations in what must be done to meet each standard. On that last date, the assessment is scheduled. I give students indicated practice, activities, and time to prepare for the assessment within this unit. Students may work on this at any time within the weeks given. There is no day-by-day itinerary that students must follow.

Students own the classroom. They have free range to use anything in the room for aiding them in learning. Rulers, markers, whiteboards, and numerous other supplies are always readily available with no permission needed to use. Students routinely will use the whiteboards to teach each other or to make their own examples.

(Continued)

(Continued)

Students support each other within this environment. There is no punishment for failure. Failure is welcomed and used as a way to learn from your mistakes. This is why I do not collect or grade any piece of practice. I use practice work, activities, projects, etc. as a way to formatively assess students, providing them with feedback to improve. Students complete the work not because of a compliance, but because they need it to learn the concepts as laid out in the expectations. When the focus is put on the learning rather than earning something for a grade, students rise to the challenge. The only work I collect and grade are their summative assessments.

> Students complete the work not because of a compliance, but because they need it to learn the concepts as laid out in the expectations.

Assessments

Students have choice when preparing and taking assessments. Before every assessment, students can independently study the concepts they need most help on. I provide students with numerous practice concepts, and students can choose to do as much or little as they want to help them prepare. Many students also create problems for each other to solve in preparation for the test. Again, I am looking for learning and not compliance in completing a review guide or worksheet.

Students can choose the date when they want to take the assessment. I set the date by which I would like students to have taken the assessment. It is not uncommon, though, for a quarter to a half of the class to take the test sooner. This allows students the flexibility to continue on with the curriculum without waiting for others. Some students also need an extra day or two in order to take the assessment. I would rather wait a couple more days for a student to be prepared for a test than to demand they take it with the rest of the class only to know they are going to perform poorly.

By giving students choice in their own education, they take ownership in what they learn. They help each other, and it provides students with a rich, meaningful environment that requires them to do their best. Constant growth is happening in this fast-paced and noisy environment.

Photos of a Differentiated Math Learning Environment

iStockphoto.com/mediaphotos

iStockphoto.com/kali9

iStockphoto.com/Antonio_Diaz

Example 5: Use Choice to Allow Students to Work at Their Own Pace

Skeptics of Kirk's model often cite things like, "you only teach the honors students" or "that only works with older children." Well, to dissuade such thoughts, let me offer another account from an elementary teacher from the same school district, Deerfield School District 109. Larissa Thurman has also found ways to include student voice and choice appropriately in her third-grade classroom of mixed-ability students. Similar to Kirk's classroom, when you walk into Larissa's classroom, students are actively engaged in a variety of types of learning: individual, small groups, and direct instruction. Below Larissa explains how she sets her students up for success using their voice in addition to formative assessment to drive learning.

Teacher Voice

Larissa Thurman, Third-Grade Teacher

Kipling Elementary School

Deerfield, IL

I'm sure that any experienced teacher would agree with me when I say that teaching math at the elementary level can be very challenging. With various styles of learning and a wide range of abilities, many teachers, including myself, have struggled with how to reach all of the different needs represented in a group of students. I found myself making sacrifices here and compromises there because I couldn't quite figure out how to teach in a way that truly allowed *all* of my students to reach their maximum potential. After several years of trying this and that, I finally feel like I have a system that provides true differentiation and student choice in my math block.

I found that guided math provided me with the opportunity to meet with smaller groups of students to provide differentiated instruction, while other groups were practicing skills through playing games and working on tasks. Although I felt this was definitely a step in the right direction, there was still something missing, not to mention I was overwhelmed by the amount of preparation I was doing on a daily basis. I knew there had to be a better way.

After meeting with my instructional coaches, observing several teachers in my district, and working with my team, it finally hit me. What if students could work on a leveled pathway that included a variety of ways to practice skills? They could work at their own pace, choose how to represent their thinking, and decide if they wanted to work on their own, with a partner, or in a small group. With students engaged in this independent work, I would be provided with more time to work with individuals and small groups to reinforce, reteach, and support various needs authentically and fluidly.

So, what does this look like and how does it work? First, I looked for resources and materials that included a variety of tasks and problems correlated to the Common Core State Standards (CCSS). I also made sure that I was using materials that would challenge students' thinking and require them to apply the Standards for Mathematical Practices. For each unit, I created several pathways, according to the needs of my students, using the third-, fourth-, fifth-, and sometimes sixth-grade CCSS. Each pathway includes a list of Khan Academy videos, which students can use as a reference for new skills, some basic skill practice, a few hands-on activities and various word problems and real-world tasks. Using assessment data, including Measures of Academic Progress (MAP), unit pre-tests, and daily performance observations, I am able to determine which pathway each student will start the unit.

With the pathways created and assigned, students are set up to be independent as they work on skills that are differentiated and challenging, which frees up my time to be able to work with small groups and individuals to provide targeted instruction. I begin each day with a short 10- to 15-minute mini-lesson introducing or practicing a new skill according to the third-grade CCSS that we are working on in the unit. I include the use of visuals and manipulatives and keep the lesson moving quickly to maintain a high level of engagement, especially for my students working above grade level. For most lessons, I use an exit ticket, a short problem that students have to complete before moving on to their pathway work, in order to assess my student's progress toward mastery of the material. This formative assessment also helps me to determine which students require extra support or reteaching, which is done while the rest of the class is working on their pathways. In doing this, I am able to provide authentic and timely support and gear my instruction to exactly what my students need in the moment.

The success of this method has translated into higher test scores on summative assessments as well as end of the year MAP testing. Since I have been using pathways, more time is spent by all of my students working on math that is meaningful and challenging, and I have the ability to reach *all* of my students' individual needs.

Example 6: Use Choice to Promote Student Autonomy and Student Efficacy

Oscar Wilde once said, "imitation is the sincerest form of flattery," and a few years ago, I flattered seventh- and eighth-grade ELA teacher Mike Taglia by imitating a learning opportunity he created for his students, which culminated in a student film festival held at a local theater.

Mike used the film festival as an authentic learning opportunity for a narrative writing unit, and my colleagues and I created a provisional version of the film festival where students created documentaries or public service announcements for an informational text/persuasive writing unit. By using the carrot of an authentic audience, and by allowing student choice and voice to drive learning, students master the learning intentions and leave eighth grade with an increased feeling of autonomy and efficacy.

Teacher Voice

Mike Taglia, Seventh- and Eighth-Grade ELA and Broadcasting Teacher

Lincoln Middle School

Park Ridge, IL

As a middle school language arts and broadcasting teacher for 22 years, the main thing I've learned is to create curriculum that matters. Curriculum that students connect with and that they feel has a purpose.

As assessment for learning and specifically pre-assessment has illustrated, each student has a different starting point and, therefore, should naturally have a different outcome. With that understanding, I've realized the most important part of educating students is the learning process and not the final outcome. However, when a teacher can include an authentic audience as part of the outcome, students' starting places become a non-issue. All students know the place where they are headed and generally want to get there.

Learning Intentions

I keep the same students for seventh and eighth grade. One of the first things I talk about in seventh grade is actually the last thing we do in eighth grade: a film unit. It's a culminating unit that incorporates the different elements of narrative story in which students write, film, and edit a short narrative film. I tell my students that it's story coming to life. I start pumping up the idea that the top movies will be played at the local movie theater at the end of the unit. We call it the Lincoln Film Fest. Awards are given out at the theater as well. As I teach and reinforce the different elements of story throughout the 2 years (plot line, characterization, foreshadowing, etc.), I remind them that these will be important aspects of the film they will eventually produce at the end of eighth grade.

Brainstorming

At the beginning of eighth grade, students choose production company groups consisting of two to five students within their class. The day before any break (Thanksgiving, Winter, Spring) is dedicated to a brainstorming session. Allowing that time for the brainstorm helps the ideas develop and grow at a slow simmer instead of simply trying to come up with an idea at the beginning of the unit in just a day or two. The first brainstorm session is an open-ended brainstorm with a focus on the type of film genre that will best fit their group. The second session focuses on the conflict. The third session focuses on characters. Each group member must provide a character sketch for his or her character in the film.

Choosing Roles

During the last 4 weeks of school, we officially begin the unit. The first thing the group members do is choose their roles for their production company. There are five roles: head writer, director, editor, creative director, and cinematographer. I go over the definitions and responsibilities for each role. I stress that they should consider their individual strengths and interests when deciding roles. As a homework assignment, students must come up with their top two role choices with a rationale as to why they believe that should be their role. The next day the members discuss their choices and rationales. As a group, they decide on roles. Typically, I agree with the role selection as group members generally understand each other's strengths and interests. If there's an obvious mismatch or a standstill within the group, I will gently guide members to roles that would be suited for them by asking a series of questions rather than telling or assigning.

Sharing Knowledge

Once roles are decided, the head writer has 3–4 days to write the narrative story using the brainstorming outlines and character sketches previously developed on the brainstorming days earlier in the year. During

(Continued)

(Continued)

Lisa Westman: The same thing happened when my colleagues and I did the documentary film festival. Students would pack the computer labs before and after school to research or work on production. The Friday afternoon when finalists were announced (using student and teacher input via a rubric) produced hallways full of students congratulating each other and reserving tickets for the show.

that time, the other group members begin researching their production roles. I've used Edmodo as an online tool in which groups are created. What I've found to be very effective is to put the groups together across all of the classes. In other words, all of the cinematographers will share one group from my four language arts classes. In those groups, members must link one video and one article about their specific production role. This provides a classroom database for each role. Students will then use class time to view the videos and read the articles to strengthen their knowledge of their roles. They are also required to comment on a certain number of videos and articles about things they've learned from them. This is when I start seeing a lot of authentic engagement. Students who only have 4 weeks left of their middle school careers are very focused for two reasons: They are interested to learn about and implement their production roles in the film, and they also want the film shown at the film fest at the local theater. The buy in is huge.

Collaborating

As the directors, editors, creative directors, and cinematographers learn about their production roles using the classroom databases, I work with the head writers conferencing with them in class and also commenting on their Google Drive document. Once the narrative story is complete, the class comes back together as a whole, and I teach script writing. The head writers will then turn the narrative story into a script focusing on the dialogue between characters. The directors will add in the characters' actions and emotions. The creative directors will add in the wardrobe, settings, props, and music. The cinematographers will add in the camera angles and lighting that they feel will best tell the story. And the editors will add in the transitions, sound and video effects, and titles. Once the script has all of those components, the group performs a table read. This is where they discuss and modify the different aspects of the script. Then it's time to film.

Filming and Editing

The filming is typically done outside of class time within a 2-week period. That time frame can be a challenge. Part of the director's job is to set the calendar of filming days that outlines where and when to meet. We've used Google calendar in the past. I stress that the script should be at the filming even though things may be revised as you film. I also stress that members must perform their roles during the filming. Directors must direct. Cinematographers must be in charge of camera angles and lighting, etc. Part of their final grade is a self-assessment about their role performance. As the film is edited in class, and I have questions, concerns, or praise about how it is evolving, I go directly to the person in charge of that aspect of the production. It brings a sense of responsibility to their production roles. They choose their own roles and are expected to implement them effectively to help tell their story.

Outcome

Every group wants their film to make it to the local theater for the film fest. That is what makes the authentic audience such a powerful tool for producing quality final outcomes. However, only about a third of the films make it to the film fest. Since it's a field trip, we have limited time there. After the films are shown, we give out awards for best actor, actress, cinematography, writing, music, editing, and best film. When we get back from the film fest, I send an email to all staff and students with a link to all of the films made that year. I include notes next to the titles for those that made the film fest and the award winners. This gives all of the groups a chance for their films to be seen and for them to feel a sense of authentic audience. A lot of teachers, during that last week, will show the films in class.

Whether students make the film fest or not, I believe in this unit for the many lessons they learn from it. It makes them dig deep into the elements of story as well as understand the subtleties of storytelling through the different production roles. And it also allows them to work in a real-world situation with specific roles, deadlines, and natural consequences. I try to model that same idea of voice and choice with an authentic audience in other units I teach. This structure is highly effective at producing student ownership of their learning.

Lack of Choice Can Inhibit Creativity

In many third- and fourth-grade classrooms across the country, students engage in an Invention Convention where they create their own invention.

In my experience, there is little (if any) research involved in these projects and certainly not a whole lot of room for students to truly drive the learning.

I once worked with a third-grade teacher who pulled a worksheet off of Pinterest to give students to help them brainstorm ideas for an invention, which they then had to create a prototype for and put their planning process on a trifold board to present to parents.

The teacher had a couple of students who were frustrated with this assignment to the point of tears and were refusing to do the work. The teacher was confused as to why the students were so frustrated. I asked her if she had asked her students why, and her response was, no. So, we asked them. It turns out, the students all had similar responses, "I can't draw my idea on paper." The worksheet, while well-intentioned, was inhibiting the students' learning process.

Instead of using the worksheet, we tried allowing student voice to drive the process. By doing so, the teacher was better able to differentiate the process and product for many of the students. Instead of creating a tangible product, one student, we'll call him Andre, made a commercial instead because his research showed that was more likely to resonate with his audience. To create his commercial, Andre needed to find out more information than the original worksheet had asked for. Therefore, he wound up going much deeper in his learning by creating a market research survey (see Figure 8.8).

Andre wanted to create a bundle package of subscriptions for apps for Apple users. We created a set of questions to guide his product development. His teacher gave him feedback each time he answered a question and then gave him an additional question. You can see the questions and his answers in Figure 8.7.

Figure 8.7   Invention Convention: Incorporating Student Voice

1. List all of the subscriptions you would like to include and the price per year.

Subscription Name	Subscription Price per Year
iTunes Match	$24.99
Picmonkey	$30.00
Applecare for all Apple devices	$83.00
Netflix	$24.99

2. What is the total price of all of these subscriptions?

   $133.00

3. List the reasons why a consumer (buyer) would want this subscription (the kids and the parents):

Parents	Kids
To easily access music	To listen to music and watch movies that their parents might have bought
To make pictures look good	To make YouTube/Facebook background art
To save money on repairs for Apple devices	To save money on repairs for Apple devices
It's more convenient and efficient for parents to only pay once.	To collaborate with other people on projects

4. Why would Apple and the other companies be interested in offering this package? How would it benefit them?

   It will get the other companies (other than apple) more business.

5. What would make Apple want to do this?

   By bundling Applecare with iTunes match, you'll sell more iTunes match.

Figure 8.8   Andre's Market Research Survey

How much would you pay?

* Required

What would be the most you would pay for a package of subscriptions including PicMonkey, Applecare, iTunes Match, and Netflix? If bought separately they would cost a total of $133.
*

○ $100.00

○ $110.00

○ $120.00

○ I would not buy this package for my family.

SUBMIT

Figure 8.9   Andre's Market Research Results

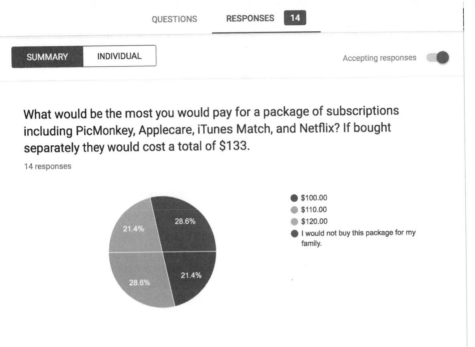

Figure 8.10   Invention Convention Product: Andre's Bundle
Commercial

By allowing Andre to stray from using the worksheet template, he was better able to communicate his ideas in a manner that was more relevant to him and authentic to his audience. And he still accomplished all of the learning intentions and success criteria established by his teacher.

Discussion Questions

▶ What role does choice play in student-driven differentiation?

▶ Why is it necessary that choice aligns to the learning intentions?

▶ How can the paradox of choice present a problem for students?

▶ How does choice promote creativity?

Visit the companion website at http://resources.corwin .com/studentdrivendifferentiation.

Chapter 9

Your Journey With Student-Driven Differentiation

"Doing is the crucible of change."

—Fullan (2011, p. 3)

We Are Entrusted With Instilling the Desire to Learn

If you were stranded on a desert island and could only take three possessions, what would you take? I really hate that question. There are *way more* than three items I would take with me if I were stranded on a desert island for an undefined amount of time. But, if I *had* to choose three items (assuming people and pets are not considered possessions), I would bring (1) my copy of Malcolm Gladwell's *Outliers*, (2) my copy of Daniel Pink's *Drive*, and (3) my journal and pen (the pen is part of the journal, so this counts as a single item).

Why these three items? The books would remind me that I am in control of my own destiny and can achieve my goals, and the journal would help me reflect on my successes and obstacles.

In case you haven't read *Outliers* or *Drive*, I'll give you the premises. In *Outliers,* Malcolm Gladwell defines the 10,000-hour rule, which says that with 10,000 hours of correct practice, one can become an expert at anything (singing, playing a sport, writing, accounting, etc.). Gladwell

Autonomy—The desire to be self-directed.

Mastery—The desire to learn or refine skills through setting and achieving goals.

Purpose—The desire to do something that makes a difference.

supports his theory with research and irrefutable examples (Gladwell, 2013). In *Drive: The Surprising Truth About What Motivates Us*, Daniel Pink provides a compelling research-based argument that true motivation is intrinsic and comes from a sense of autonomy, mastery, and purpose. Therefore, to ensure members of an organization (in this case students and teachers) are truly motivated, we must focus on creating conditions that foster these characteristics. Conversely, we must do-away with extrinsic motivators like grades, money, rewards, and punishments (Pink, 2009).

When we synthesize the premises of both books, we gain a very important message about our professional work as educators, specifically in regard to student-driven differentiation which I summarize like this. As educators, we are entrusted with one of the most difficult yet most worthwhile tasks: ensuring that all students learn and more importantly *want to continue learning* when they leave our classrooms. To accomplish this feat, we must allow ourselves to be learners, to set meaningful professional goals, take the time to perfect the steps to achieve our goals, and to reflect upon our successes and struggles in an effort to set new goals and build our efficacy—individually and collectively.

> As educators, we are entrusted with one of the most difficult yet most worthwhile tasks: ensuring that all students learn and more importantly *want to continue learning* when they leave our classrooms.

Things to keep in mind as you set your goal:

- The big four are classroom management, content, instruction, and assessment (Knight, 2007)
- Assessment evidence, including assessments that consider student voice, should drive your goal.
- Set a measurable goal.
- Set a feasible goal.
- Set a goal that builds upon your strengths.
- Step out of your comfort zone!

Collective efficacy: an attitude amongst teachers in a school that together they can make a difference for students

We Are Better Together: Collective Efficacy

Collective efficacy has the number one effect size on student performance (Donohoo, 2017, p. 3; Hattie, 2017).

In *Collective Efficacy,* Jenni Donohoo outlines four sources (based on the research of psychologist Albert Bandura) that can build efficacy amongst teachers:

1. **Mastery experiences:** Individuals or teams experience success and recognize the success came from their actions and want to engage in additional, similar experiences.

2. **Vicarious experiences:** when we see others have success with challenges

3. **Social persuasion:** encouragement from credible educators or influencers that we can be successful

4. **Affective states:** feelings toward one's own competence (Donohoo, 2017, p. 8)

These four sources can all be actualized when you decide to incorporate student-driven differentiation, as I will detail in this chapter.

Mastery Experience: Set Goals to Increase Efficacy

Just as students can take ownership of their learning through goal setting, adult educators can do the same. And, the tenets of goal-setting do not change: goals should be emotionally compelling, feasible, attainable, and have clear criteria for mastery.

I also argue that professional goals should always be optional, never mandatory. Many school systems begin each year with well-intentioned plans that mandate teachers set goals for themselves. Think of the opening institute day: after a long day of learning, teachers are asked to complete an exit slip with their goal for the school year, and teachers (myself included) hurriedly scribble down a goal on a slip of paper before running back to their classrooms to ready it for their students first day. This *is not* the type of goal setting I am talking about. In fact, as Derek Sivers points out in his TED Talk, *Keep Your Goals to Yourself* (2010), multiple psychological studies (1926: Lewin, 1933: Wera, 1982, 2009: Gollwitzer) show that goals created in haste and shared socially (as on an exit slip) fool the brain into thinking they already accomplished the goal just by sharing it—a phenomenon called social reality.

Emotionally compelling goals created after significant thought, however, have the opposite effect. What I am referring to are those goals that come from situations that keep you up at night—a difficult class (set a classroom management goal), students not contributing to class discussion (set an instruction goal), students not making growth (set an assessment goal). As established in Chapter 2, almost all professional goals that are set using evidence of student performance (including their voice) *will result* in student-driven differentiation.

Goal-setting and creating appropriate action plans during these emotionally charged situations will alleviate stress, and when the goal is actualized in a mastery experience, your efficacy will be built.

As an instructional coach, I recommend you partner with an instructional coach to help you identify the correct goal, strategies to achieve the goal, and data to determine whether or not the strategies are effective. However, I recognize that due to logistical constraints working with an instructional coach is not always possible. If this is the case, the next best option is to partner with a colleague to help you set a goal and hold you accountable to a certain extent. Or, if all else fails, set your own goals, and hold yourself accountable. Be sure to set a goal that is right for you and your students. The goal-setting guide below can help with this process (adapted from instructional coaching techniques via Jim Knight). The questions are general questions, and the blue italicized responses serve as an example.

Vicarious Experiences: Observe Teachers in Action

In his column, *Finding Common Ground*, Peter DeWitt addresses this second way of building collective efficacy:

> Bandura's research shows we learn best through vicarious experiences, where we can observe others in action. Those experiences may take place when we observe another teacher's classroom, co-teach with another teacher, or learn from them when we share best practices around a given strategy at a faculty meeting. Versland (2016) found that, "If the successful person appears to be of similar competence to the vicarious learner, the vicarious learner seeks to replicate the efforts and strategies to achieve similar success." (DeWitt, 2017b)

As teachers and leaders, we need more of those vicarious experiences in our lives. Guskey (1986) says that we need to offer professional learning and development opportunities that will offer teachers a new strategy that they can use immediately; they must use it and see student growth quickly, and then their beliefs will change. He writes, "significant change in teachers' beliefs and attitudes is likely to take place only after changes in student learning outcomes are evidenced" (Guskey, 1986; as quoted in DeWitt, 2017b).

Figure 9.1   Student-Driven Differentiation Goal-Setting Guide

What is my goal/what do I want to accomplish?
I want to strengthen my rapport with students.

How will student learning improve with this goal?
If students and I have a stronger working relationship, I believe they will perform better on formative assessments because they will be more likely to ask me questions and receive helpful answers.

How will I know when I have reached my goal?
I will increase the number of approachable verbal and nonverbal signals I give to students and the ratio of teacher/student comments will be 50/50 or better (in favor of the students).

What will look different if I accomplish my goal?
I will engage in respectful and productive conversations with students.

What steps will I take to reach my goal?

I will use cooperative learning structures to promote discussion and ask more questions than give directives. I will work with a colleague to take data on my verbal and nonverbal cues and the number of questions/comments I make. I will video record lessons to take my data and compare with the data my colleague takes on the same lesson using a data collection tool we co-create.

How often will I check to see if I am progressing toward my goal?
Once a week until my goal is met, then once a month to ensure sustainability.

Expanding the walls of the classroom applies to teachers as well as students. We can use Skype/Google Hangout to observe classrooms around the world.

DeWitt's post supports the notion of professional goal setting and action plans and encourages adding meaningful observations of others as a means to see that our goals are achievable. It wasn't until I became an instructional coach, and I was observing teachers with specific criteria in mind, that I recognized the true power of peer observation and recognized what I was observing. And, at that point, all I wanted to do was create a wall that celebrated something extraordinary I saw in each and every classroom. And this is one way I think we can help build each other's efficacy through impacting their affective state (more on this in a bit) and also providing opportunities for vicarious learning opportunities.

What I suggest is somewhat of a reverse pineapple chart approach. The pineapple chart is a popular system of professional learning that allows teachers to invite one another into their classrooms for informal observation. For a more detailed description and a sample of a pineapple chart, see Jennifer Gonzalez's 2017 piece, *How Pineapple Charts Revolutionize Professional Development*. Post the chart in a common location: the teacher's lounge, the copy room, hallway, etc. I propose that we create charts collectively. Rather than promoting ourselves or inviting others into our classrooms to see a certain activity, we collectively identify all of the things we want to do and would like to see others do (aka our goals) and hang the chart in a visible place. Then, as we observe each other's classrooms, we can indicate where we saw specific examples of practices that support our goals. As a coach, I would certainly be able to add every teacher's name to one box on the chart, and my hope is that building administrators would be able to do the same. Together, we create a visual reminder of teachers' efficacy and a list of potential vicarious learning experiences. Below, I have created an example of this using some of this book's vignette contributors as examples.

Social Persuasion: Inspire Through Storytelling

Stories can be told spontaneous or planned. They can be personal accounts, analogies, or classics. Whatever type of story is included, they should be simple, conversational, concise, and appropriately paced.

The third way to build efficacy is through social persuasion, which is a fancy way to say inspiration from others who are credible (and often inspirational). There are a variety of people who can fill this role: colleagues, administrators, authors, presenters, etc.

For the purpose of this book, I want to offer you one last compelling reason to implement student-driven differentiation in the form of a story. As an added bonus, you can also adapt this story to use with your students as a hook or part of a lesson.

Figure 9.2   Reverse Pineapple Chart

Cooperative Learning	**Feedback**	**Student Goal Setting**
Cathy—See how her students use rally coach with performance assessments.	Jim—Ask him to see how he used one student's mastery of a standard to benefit the whole class.	Samantha—I saw her setting MAP goals with her students. Now I know how to do this!
Flexible Pacing	**Solid Hook**	**Student Ownership of Learning**
Kirk—Did you know students determine when they are ready to be formatively and summatively assessed in Kirk's class?	Diane—I was so engaged in the video Diane showed her students, I wanted to personally participate in the activity!	Jeff—He has a great model of goal setting, creating action plans, and conferring with students which allows them full control over their learning.

Storytelling (personal, fictional, analogous) is a versatile and (when done correctly) powerful instructional strategy that accomplishes several things in the classroom:

- Anchoring new knowledge

- Building prior knowledge

- Prompting thinking and dialogue

- Generating interest

- Inspiring hope

- Offering new perspectives (Knight, 2013, pp. 182–183).

My favorite story is *The Wizard of Oz* written by Frank Baum in 1900, and it just so happens that *The Wizard of Oz* is analogous to implementing student-driven differentiation.

On the surface, *The Wizard of Oz* is a simple tale about a girl and her friends on a journey, but in actuality, many people argue that the story is about much more than that. Some argue that it is an economic allegory of the United States at the turn of the 20th century. They claim that the characters and symbols represent economic forces. Some examples are listed in Figure 9.3.

From my perspective, *The Wizard of Oz* can also be an allegory for implementing student-driven differentiation. We educators are Dorothy trying to follow the Yellow Brick Road (implementing student-driven differentiation). Sometimes, we get lost or face a formidable foe (the witch). But the answer

Figure 9.3   Symbolism in *The Wizard of Oz*

Character/Symbol	Represents
Dorothy	Average American Citizen
Scarecrow	Farmers
Tinman	Industrial workers
Lion	William Jennings Bryan, leader of the populist party and silver movement leader
Emerald City	Washington D.C. and its focus on money/all things green
Oz	Abbreviation for gold
Yellow Brick Road	The Gold Standard
Munchkins	Citizens of the east who wanted to keep the Gold Standard in place
Silver Slippers (Ruby slippers in the movie)	The answer was right under the citizen's nose: adding silver to the economy

Source: Silverstein (2015)

is always right under our noses. The way back to the Yellow Brick Road is recognizing that we

1. may struggle. We may make mistakes along the way, and that is ok. This is how we grow and learn. We are knowledge workers, and we use our *brains* to guide us. Growing brains is what we want.

2. use student voice to drive our instructional decisions because we take our students' needs (academic, social-emotional, and otherwise) to *heart.* We know the surefire way to reach all of our students is to partner with them in the learning process and honor their individual and collective voices.

3. can change our direction through the knowledge gained in the process of learning. This is not always easy; there are sometimes obstacles which we must face, but as educators who care about students, we have the *courage* to face these obstacles, find resources, collaborate with others, and overcome these hurdles.

Affective States: Support Fellow Educators Through Positive Communication

Affective states refer to individual's feelings toward their own competence or perceived lack thereof. Affective states of individuals make up the climate or culture of an educational organization (Donohoo, 2017, p. 8). While affective states are less impactful on efficacy than mastery experiences or vicariously learning, they are yet another way our individual actions can spread to others for good or for bad.

One of the most effective and energy-conserving practices we can engage in to promote positive affective states is by engaging in productive and positive conversations rather than unproductive and toxic conversations. I address positive conversations in detail in this recent blog post:

The Three Biggest Time Killers We Do Little to Avoid

by Lisa Westman

May 24, 2017

Finding Common Ground

blogs.edweek.org

Teachers overwhelmingly cite time (76% of those surveyed) as the thing they wish they had more of each day (Gates Foundation, 2014). Teachers want additional time to assess student work, plan lessons, and meet with colleagues. On the flipside, staff meetings, professional development, and logistical tasks are listed as inefficient uses of time.

There are additional contributors that collectively kill as much or more time that are under teachers' direct control, and yet little is done to address or change these practices. What I am referring to are our conversations: in the hallway, in the lounge, in meetings.

Conversations and Better Conversations

Last week marked the end of a year-long, intensive instructional coaching workshop led by Jim Knight. While the workshop focused on instructional coaching, much of the content applies to life in general; my learning from the workshop positively impacted both my professional and personal life.

Case in point, the lessons I learned on how to communicate more effectively with others. In Knight's session on better conversations (based

(Continued)

(Continued)

on the book by the same name), Knight (2016) outlines the steps we should take to improve as conversation partners. These criteria ultimately lead to increased productivity and camaraderie. Knight includes an entire chapter on the importance of finding common ground with those whom we converse. Knight suggests using the acronym ICARE (interests, convictions, activities, roles, experiences) to help us identify safe categories we can explore with our conversation partners to find similarities.

What if we find common ground, but the bonds are destructive?

Since the workshop on Better Conversations, I have keenly observed others engaged in conversation to see how they find common ground with their colleagues.

I have seen many positive examples of people connecting through ICARE conversations about favorite sports teams, graduate school classes, and weekend plans.

Conversely, I have also seen people finding common ground in non-ICARE ways (including me). Whether conversation partners are aware of this or not, many people find common ground rooted in judgment, gossip, or negativity. These likenesses certainly do not garner positive outcomes, and frankly they are an unwise use of our most coveted commodity—time.

Judgment

"There doesn't seem to be a lot of structure at home."

"I know. Johnny came to school without his homework log signed for the third week in a row."

Judgment is a sheep in wolf's clothing. People often engage in this type of talk and feel as if they have found solid common ground. After all, this is a discussion between two people who share a common belief (it is important for students to comply with teacher orders), which appears to be rooted in the best interest of children.

However, there is an underlying judgment of the students' parents here (they aren't doing what they need to do). Additionally, there is a judgment of the student (he should still comply even though he may not have the same opportunities to do so). And, frankly, this type of conversation is not productive. Yet, week after week, year after year, some teachers will continue to engage in conversations which are founded in judgment without consideration of what can be done to alleviate the problem.

Gossip

"Did you hear that teacher is being reassigned?"

"Yes, I heard that. But, I am not surprised. She really struggled this year, and I heard there were a lot of parent complaints about her."

As Jane Austen once said, "Every man is surrounded by a neighborhood of voluntary spies." These "spies" are quick to share their observations in an effort to preserve their own status. Gossip does not help the subject (what could have been done to help this struggling teacher earlier in the year), and gossiping immediately extinguishes trust. If you gossip about one person, everyone knows there is a chance you will one day gossip about them, too. Without trust, productivity is compromised, and again time is wasted.

Negativity

"Students have no accountability anymore. They are in for a rude awakening in the real world when there are no retakes."

"I know. Every year we keep lowering our standards for students."

Negativity may be the most pervasive conversation killer and it is also highly contagious. Negativity places blame and focuses on problems rather than promoting ownership and a focus on solutions. Simply, negativity brings everyone down, including our students.

In the End

Judgment, gossip, and negativity are a part of life. From time to time we all engage in conversations which allow us to vent. And this is ok. The key is recognizing when these practices are habitual and destructive and that change must occur. That change starts with us.

Few people volunteer to step up and redirect toxic conversations. Many of us try to avoid conflict and fear repercussions. Plus, it can be uncomfortable to be the voice of dissent, even though the dissenting voice is positive.

How do you feel when you mitigate your feelings and allow toxic conversations to continue? I wind up feeling safe in the moment, but terrible after the fact. To find a happy medium, I employ the three suggestions below to safely redirect judgment, gossip, and negativity.

(Continued)

(Continued)

▶ **Be Proactive:** Bring up your concerns, but make them about yourself (even if it is really about someone else). "I was wondering if you could help me. I noticed that I pass judgment on the families and students who don't complete homework and I don't like this feeling. I can imagine you feel the same way. How can we work together to better address our students' needs?"

▶ **Excuse yourself:** When gossip rears its ugly head; our tendencies are to either join in or to listen, but not participate. However, silence can indicate consent and give gossipers an unspoken thumbs up. To stop gossip, we need to remove outlets. Therefore, create a mental bank of excuses which you can use to remove yourself from gossipy conversations, "Oh, I left something in the teacher workroom. . . . Sorry to cut you off, I need to use the washroom before my students get back from their electives. . . . I am about to go meet with so-so, can we talk later?"

▶ **Kindly state an alternate point of view:** I recognize this can be hard to do. As stated, negativity is contagious. If someone sneezed, you would offer them a tissue or move away from them to protect yourself. We need to treat negativity the same way. Acknowledge your colleague's point of view and kindly share another perspective, "I understand what you are saying. It can be frustrating when students take longer to learn, and we need to reteach. But, since our job is to ensure all students succeed, what is the alternative?" If all else fails, go back to suggestion number two and excuse yourself.

How else do you seek to find common ground with your colleagues? What successful strategies have you used and what other obstacles have you encountered and how have you worked to overcome these barriers?

Now What? Summing It All Up

While growing up, my father frequently shared proverbs. One of the sayings that resonated with me most was "integrity is a full-time job." When it comes to student-driven differentiation, *our* integrity to the process, to our students, to our colleagues, and to ourselves is of upmost importance.

There will be both triumphs and struggles. How we choose to respond will determine our individual and collective success using student-driven differentiation to ensure all of our students have appropriate opportunities to learn, grow, and achieve. When we feel discouraged, we need to remember our purpose, remember we are still learners ourselves, and that mastery takes time and effort. We can model the traits we aim to see in our students (motivation, creativity, curiosity, tenacity) by demonstrating them in our own professional growth.

> "Integrity is a full-time job."

In *Visible Learning for Teachers*, John Hattie urges teachers to "know thy impact" (2012). There are many ways to determine our impact (test scores, parent emails, tokens of appreciation during teacher appreciation week), but, perhaps, there is no greater way of knowing our impact and respecting student voice than asking the students about your impact and accepting the answers as formative assessment for our own growth. If we have 20 students, and 19 of them provide affirming feedback, but one student gives us a more critical response, we have a hint of where to go next.

Rudyard Kipling best described how we should proceed on our professional and personal paths in his poem, "If." Kipling wrote the poem for his son offering him the characteristics a man should possess. We can apply some of the sentiments in our journey to educate all our students:

"If" by Rudyard Kipling

If you can dream—and not make dreams your master . . .

If you can think—and not make thoughts your aim;

If you can meet with triumph and disaster, and treat those two impostors just the same;

If you can make one heap of all your winning, and risk it on one turn of pitch-and-toss,

And lose, and start again at your beginnings, and never breathe a word about your loss . . .

If we can remain ourselves, true to our students, and true to each other, together we will create the most magnificent symphony.

Discussion Questions

▶ How do autonomy, mastery, and purpose impact professional learning? How do they impact student learning?

▶ How have you personally experienced efficacy building with mastery experiences, vicarious learning experiences, social persuasion, and/or affective states?

▶ How does goal setting lead to mastery experiences?

▶ How can you incorporate vicarious learning experiences into your professional practice?

▶ How can storytelling be an impactful instructional strategy for both adult and child learners?

▶ How will you avoid or discourage judgement, gossip, and negativity in your school system?

Visit the companion website at http://resources.corwin .com/studentdrivendifferentiation.

Afterword

In the spring of 2007, the teachers and administration of Woodstock High School in Illinois faced a crossroads. We reached the decision that offering remedial courses in English, social studies, and science was antithetical to our dreams of developing a high-performing and equitable high school. While confident in our decision on educational and moral grounds, the nagging questions persisted of how to eliminate remedial courses and what should instructional spaces in our school look like with more heterogeneous classrooms. How could we provide greater challenges to a segment of our students who were certainly capable but had been withheld from more rigorous experiences?

As the principal at that time, all eyes were on me. What are we going to do, Mr. Principal? The beauty of working with people smarter than you is that when collaboration, a moral imperative, and a spark of urgency are combined, you can sometimes discover a touch of brilliance. After long debate, we decided the key to our path forward rested in our ability to strengthen the staff's ability to provide differentiated instruction. Looking back on that decision, we were both right and wrong.

We felt that once we had chosen our path toward this academic advancement through differentiated instruction, we should be set, and everything would fall into place. Surprisingly, after we had researched and assessed the best method to provide professional development for our staff, we didn't have many good options, and we lost some confidence in our direction. There seemed to be a vacuum of information on how we could develop an instructional system that could provide each student with both the challenge and support needed through differentiated experiences.

In the end, our highly successful initiative had nothing to do with the trainer we brought in or the strategies we learned during the professional development that followed. The success of this initiative came back to two important characteristics that are addressed in this book *Student-Driven Differentiation*—*relationships* and *expectations*. Our staff succeeded at differentiating classroom experiences for children because we created a systemic culture of care for our students combined with an unwavering expectancy of excellence.

If only this book had been around 10 years ago! Mrs. Westman's book prescribes exactly what we wandered into rather accidentally—a system that values not only the unique experiences of each student, but also his or her personal growth, creating engaging and enjoyable spaces for students as well as staff. When provided with voice and authentic experiences, students begin to value their powerful role, and teachers no longer see differentiated instruction as the elusive Holy Grail of education.

Culture always trumps strategy, as they say. I hope you can see the incredible power of this book not as a series of strategies, but as a method to establish a system, or a mindset, that will endure and thrive no matter the chosen instructional method for that particular student or lesson. Administrators and teachers will find a wonderful common ground on the pages of this fine book.

—Corey Tafoya, EdD, Superintendent
Harvard Community Unit School District 50
Harvard, IL

Glossary

affective states   feelings about one's own competence

assessment   methods used to determine where a student is in his or her learning

authentic   relevant to students

bias   showing an inclination or prejudice for or against someone or something

Bloom's taxonomy   categorization of levels of human learning

collective efficacy   an attitude amongst teachers in a school that together they can make a difference for students

content   what is to be learned

curriculum compacting   differentiation strategy that can benefit high-achieving students. It is a process by which evidence from pre-assessments is used to help students determine what parts of the curriculum they have already mastered.

differentiation   an approach to teaching in which educators actively plan for students' differences so that all students can best learn. In a differentiated classroom, teachers divide their time, resources, and efforts to effectively teach students who have various backgrounds, readiness and skill levels, and interests (ASCD, 2017).

direct instruction   explicit teaching of a skill set or concept

feedback   information given to students connected to learning goals that provides insight as to where they are and where they need to go next

formative assessment   check of where a student is, which informs next steps for both student learning and teacher instruction

goal setting   process of identifying what, how, and when, and/or why a student is to learn something

growth   measurement that monitors student learning and mastery of skills in comparison to themselves, not other students

hook   opening for a unit or lesson that makes the learning sticky and relevant for students

incorporating movement   embedding opportunities for students to use their gross motor skills to better stimulate their brains

learning environment   where and with whom students learn

learning intentions   skills and concepts students are to master in a lesson or unit

MAP   Measures of Academic Progress

mastery experiences   accomplishments achieved through setting and reaching goals

metacognitive needs   thinking about how one learns best and why

passion projects   inquiry-based learning opportunities for students with topics and action plans co-developed by the student and teacher

process   how students acquire information

product   how students demonstrate learning

questioning   asking students a mix of queries of various kinds and levels of difficulty that promote deep learning rather than surface learning

readiness   where a student is academically or socially-emotionally in regard to a particular learning intention

scaffold learning   supports offered to students; the practice of providing direct instruction and support for students as they acquire a skill or knowledge and gradually release the supports in place as they grow in their understanding (Wormeli & Tomlinson, 2007, p. 97)

selective mutism   inability to speak in certain situations, like at school, due to excessive shyness, fear of social embarrassment, social isolation, or withdrawal

social persuasion   encouragement through credible and trustworthy sources

standards aligned   matching learning intentions to the components of the standard

student-driven differentiation   a teaching method that shifts the focus of what students do to what students learn. Student-driven differentiation helps teachers strike a healthy balance in their relationships with all students and creates conditions for students to engage in and own learning that is appropriate for their readiness level and acquisition rate.

success criteria   item(s) that answer the question: "How will teachers and students know when the Learning Goal has been met?"

summative assessment   evaluates student learning at the end of an instructional unit

tool   anything that assists students and/or teachers in learning

vicarious experiences   observing others in similar situations experience success

Webb's Depth of Knowledge   classifies tasks according to the complexity of thinking required to successfully complete them

References

Ainsworth, L., & Viegut, D. (2015). *Common formative assessments 2.0: How teacher teams intentionally align standards, instruction, and assessment.* Thousand Oaks, CA: Corwin.

American Speech Language Hearing Association. (2017). Selective mutism. Retrieved from https://www.asha.org/public/speech/disorders/SelectiveMutism/

ASCD. (2017). Differentiated instruction. Retrieved from http://www.ascd.org/research-a-topic/differentiated-instruction-resources.aspx

Assess. (2017). *Merriam-Webster's Thesaurus.* Retrieved from https://www.merri-am-web ster.com/thesaurus/assess

Baum, L. F. (2008). *The wizard of Oz.* New York, NY: Modern Pub.

Bradbury, R. (1950). *Fahrenheit 451.* New York, NY: Simon and Schuster.

Bronson, P., & Merryman, A. (2014, January 23). *The creativity crisis.* Retrieved from http://www.newsweek.com/creativity-crisis-74665

Burnett, M. (2009–2017). (Producer) *Shark Tank* [Television series].

Cash, R. M. (2010). *Advancing differentiation: Thinking and learning for the 21st century.* Minneapolis, MN: Free Spirit Publishing.

Coil, C. (2008). What is curriculum compacting? Retrieved from http://www.carolyn coil.com/ezine21.htm

Common Core State Standards Initiative. (2017). Retrieved from http://www.corest andards.org/ELA-Literacy/W/4/2/

Consistent. (2017). *English Oxford Living Dictionaries.* Retrieved from https://en.ox forddictionaries.com/definition/consistent

Couros, G. (2015). *The innovator's mindset: Empower learning, unleash talent, and lead a culture of creativity.* San Diego, CA: Dave Burgess Consulting.

Covey, S. R. (2016). *The 7 habits of highly effective people.* Selangor, Malaysia: PTS Publishing House.

Crooks, B. (2016, July 9). What it's like to be black in Naperville, America. Facebook Post. https://www.facebook.com/brian.crooks/posts/10103901923530909

Dean, J. (2017). Retrieved from https://www.brainyquote.com/quotes/jimmy_dean_131287

Delisle, J. (2015, January 6). *Differentiation doesn't work* [Web log post]. Retrieved from http://www.edweek.org/ew/articles/2015/01/07/differentiation-doesnt-work .html

DeWitt, P. (2017a, April 9). *Can we destroy the silver bullet mentality before it destroys us?* Retrieved from http://blogs.edweek.org/edweek/finding_com mon_ground/2017/04/can_we_destroy_the_silver_bullet_mentality_before_it_destroys_us.html

DeWitt, P. (2017b, June 11). *Vicariously learning experiences: Why aren't we doing more of those?* Retrieved from http://blogs.edweek.org/edweek/finding_com

mon_ground/2017/06/vicariously_learning_experiences_why_arent_we_doing_more_of_that.html

Donohoo, J. (2017). *Collective efficacy: How educators' beliefs impact student learning.* Thousand Oaks, CA: Corwin.

Fox, J. (2008). *Your child's strengths: Discover them, develop them, use them.* New York, NY: Viking.

Fullan, M. (2013). *Stratosphere: Integrating technology, pedagogy, and change knowledge.* Don Mills, ON: Pearson.

Gates Foundation. (2014). *Primary sources: Teachers' views on common core state standards, America's teachers on teaching in an era of change.* Retrieved from http://www.scholastic.com/primarysources/PrimarySources-2014update.pdf

Gladwell, M. (2013). *Outliers: The story of success.* New York, NY: Back Bay Books, Little, Brown and Company.

Gonzalez, J. (2017, September 9). *How pineapple charts revolutionize professional development.* Retrieved from https://www.cultofpedagogy.com/pineapple-charts/

Habituation. (2017). Dictionary.com. Retrieved from http://www.dictionary.com/browse/habituation

Hattie, J. (2012). *Visible learning for teachers: Maximizing impact on learning.* London, UK: Routledge.

Hattie, J. (2017). *Hattie ranking: 195 Influences and effect sizes related to student achievement, 2017.* Retrieved from visible-learning.org/hattie-ranking-influ ences-effect-sizes-learning-achievement/

Jensen, E. (2005). *Teaching with the brain in mind* (2nd ed.) Alexandria, VA: ASCD.

Kagan, S. (2013). *Kagan cooperative learning structures: Minibook.* San Clemente, CA: Kagan Publishing.

Kipling, R., Beecroft, J., & Powers, R. M. (1956). *Kipling: A selection of his stories and poems.* Garden City, NY: Doubleday & Company.

Knight, J. (2007). *Instructional coaching: A partnership approach to improving instruction.* Thousand Oaks, CA: Corwin.

Knight, J. (2013). *High-impact instruction: A framework for great teaching.* Thousand Oaks, CA: Corwin.

Knight, J. (2016). *Better conversations: Coaching ourselves and each other to be more credible, caring, and connected.* Thousand Oaks, CA: Corwin.

Luketic, R. (Director). (2001). *Legally Blond* [Motion picture on DVD].

Meyer, D. (2010). Math class needs a makeover. Retrieved from https://www.ted.com/talks/dan_meyer_math_curriculum_makeover

Myers, V. (2014, November). How to overcome our biases? Walk boldly toward them. Retrieved from https://www.ted.com/talks/verna_myers_how_to_overcome_our_biases_walk_boldly_toward_them

Mini mock trial. (n.d.). Retrieved from www.teachingcivics.org

Northwest Evaluation Association. (2013). Measures of academic progress: A comprehensive guide to the MAP K–12 Computer Adaptive Interim Assessment. https://www.nwea.org/content/uploads/2014/07/Comprehensive-Guide-to-MAP-K-12-Computer-Adaptive-Interim-Assessment

Peters, S. J., Matthews, M., McBee, M. T., & McCoach, D. B. (2013). *Beyond gifted education: Designing and implementing advanced academic programs.* Waco, TX: Prufrock Press.

Pink, D. H. (2009). *Drive: The surprising truth about what motivates us*. New York, NY: Riverhead Books.

Quaglia, R. (2016, September 15). 2016 Quaglia Institute School Voice Report is first to present data from survey of teachers, students and parents. Retrieved from http://www.prnewswire.com/news-releases/2016-quaglia-institute-school-voice-report-is-first-to-present-data-from-survey-of-teachers-students-and-parents-300328418.html

Quaglia, R. J., & Corso, M. J. (2014). *Student voice: The instrument of change*. Thousand Oaks, CA: Corwin.

Robinson, K. (2006). Do schools kill creativity? Retrieved from https://www.ted.com/talks/ken_robinson_says_schools_kill_creativity

Schwartz, B. (2016). *The paradox of choice: Why more is less*. New York, NY: Ecco.

Silverstein, S. (2015, August 15). *Here's the real, forgotten meaning of* The Wizard of Oz. Retrieved from https://www.businessinsider.com.au/wizard-of-oz-american-economic-commentary-2015-8

Singer, T. (2015, September). Get explicit about implicit bias [Blog post]. Retrieved from https://tonyasinger.com/get-explicit-about-implicit-bias/

Sivers, D. (2010). *Keep your goals to yourself*. Retrieved from https://www.ted.com/talks/derek_sivers_keep_your_goals_to_yourself

Smith, S. J., & Hickner, S. (Directors), & Seinfeld, J. (Producer). (2007). *Bee movie* [Motion picture]. United States: Paramount Pictures.

Sprick, R. S., & Baldwin, K. (2009). *CHAMPs: A proactive & positive approach to classroom management*. Eugene, OR: Pacific Northwest Publishing.

Team ISTE. (2016). *Here's how you teach innovative thinking*. https://www.iste.org/explore/articleDetail?articleid=651

Thrively. (n.d.). http://www.thrively.com/

Tomlinson, C. A. (2014). *The differentiated classroom: Responding to the needs of all learners*. Alexandria, VA: ASCD.

US Department of Education. (2017, January). National Education Technology Plan. Retrieved from https://tech.ed.gov/netp/

United States Department of Labor. (1999). Futurework—Trends and challenges for work in the 21st century. Retrieved from https://www.dol.gov/oasam/programs/history/herman/reports/futurework/report.htm

US Bureau of Labor Statistics. (2017). *Industries at a glance*. Retrieved from https://www.bls.gov/iag/tgs/iag60.htm

Valiente, A. (2013). *The successful 'Shark Tank' Pitch: Mark Cuban's 7 tips*. Retrieved from http://abcnews.go.com/Business/successful-shark-tank-pitch-mark-cubans-tips/story?id=21282438

Watterson, B. (1993, March 29). *Calvin and Hobbes*. Retrieved from http://www.gocomics.com/calvinandhobbes/1993/03/29

Weiss, D. (2014, October 10). Possessionista Celebrity Style. Retrieved from http://www.possessionista.com/

Westman, L. (2016, October 4). Actually, I wasn't listening to anything you said. Retrieved from https://www.google.com/url?hl=en&q=http://blogs.edweek.org/edweek/finding_common_ground/2016/10/actually_i_wasnt_listening_to_anything_you_said.html&source=gmail&ust=1507939118529000&usg=AFQjC-NHRAqeU3qAgkWHAdvzPe8oNugBp3Q

Westman, L. (2017, April 20). Why differentiation misses the mark for gifted students. Retrieved from http://blogs.edweek.org/edweek/finding_common_ground/2017/04/why_differentiation_misses_the_mark_for_gifted_students.html

Westman, L. (2017, May 24). The three biggest time killers we do little to avoid. Retrieved from http://blogs.edweek.org/edweek/finding_common_ground/2017/05/the_three_biggest_time_killers_we_do_little_to_avoid.html

Wormeli, R., & Tomlinson, C. A. (2007). *Differentiation: From planning to practice, grades 6–12*. Portland, ME : Stenhouse.

Index

Figures are indicated by *fig* following the page number.

Notes

Notes

Notes

Notes

_____

_____

_____

_____

_____

_____

_____

_____

_____

_____

_____

_____

_____

_____

_____

_____

_____

_____

_____

_____

Notes

John Antonetti, Terri Stice

Analyze, design, and refine engaging tasks of learning.

ISBN: 978-1-5063-9914-0

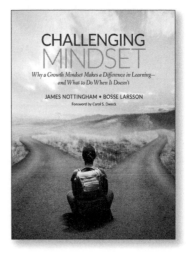

James Nottingham, Bosse Larsson

Discover strategies to encourage a growth mindset during moments of challenge in your classroom.

ISBN: 978-1-5063-7662-2

Serena Pariser

Learn from a teacher who's been through it all! Real talk about thriving and learning in the classroom.

ISBN: 978-1-5443-1775-5

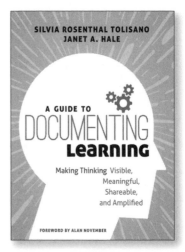

Silvia Rosenthal Tolisano, Janet A. Hale

Take a new approach to contemporary documentation and learning.

ISBN: 978-1-5063-8557-0

Corwin books represent the latest thinking from some of the most respected experts in PreK–12 education. We are proud of the breadth and depth of the books we publish and the authors we partner with in our mission to better serve educators and students.

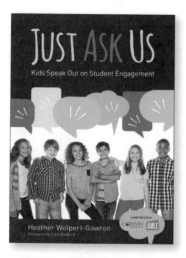

Heather Wolpert-Gawron

Use these 10 strategies to teach and communicate content that sticks!

ISBN: 978-1-5063-6328-8

Guy Claxton

Become mind-fit for life!

ISBN: 978-1-5063-8870-0

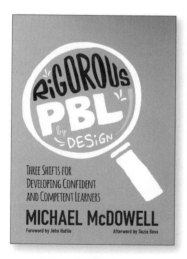

Michael McDowell

Tackle project-based learning (PBL) with real life classroom implementation and lesson plans.

ISBN: 978-1-5063-5902-1

Jayme Linton

Develop your blueprint for empowering students through personalized learning.

ISBN: 978-1-5443-1863-9

CORWIN
A SAGE Publishing Company

A SAGE Publishing Company

Helping educators make the greatest impact

CORWIN HAS ONE MISSION: to enhance education through intentional professional learning.

We build long-term relationships with our authors, educators, clients, and associations who partner with us to develop and continuously improve the best evidence-based practices that establish and support lifelong learning.